BE MY GUEST

Also by Priya Basil

Strangers on the 16:02
The Obscure Logic of the Heart
Ishq and Mushq

BE MY GUEST

PRIYA BASIL

CANONGATE

First published in Great Britain and Canada in 2019
by Canongate Books Ltd, 14 High Street, Edinburgh EH1 1TE

Distributed in Canada by Publishers Group Canada

canongate.co.uk

1

Permissions credits TK

British Library Cataloguing-in-Publication Data
A catalogue record for this book is available on
request from the British Library

ISBN 978 1 78689 849 4

Typeset in Mrs Eaves by
Palimpsest Book Production Ltd, Falkirk, Stirlingshire

Printed and bound in Great Britain by Clays Ltd, Elcograf S.p.A.

MIX
Paper from
responsible sources
FSC® C018072

TO BERLIN

We begin as guests, every single one of us. Helpless little creatures whose every need must be attended to, who for a long time can give nothing or very little back, yet who — in the usual run of things — nevertheless insinuate ourselves deep into the lives of our carers and take up permanent residence in their hearts.

Our early dependence is indulged in the expectation that we, in turn, will become dependable. Maybe reaching adulthood really means learning to be more host than guest: to take care more than, or at least as much as, to be taken care of. Implicit in this outlook, it seems to me, is still an assumption that each person will, eventually, become a parent — the ultimate role, at least in cultures where the nuclear family is considered the foundation of society. A role I decided to forego. A choice that left me questioning what my part can be in the life-play of hospitality.

Whether you have your own kids or not, it's hard to avoid the general shift from guest to host, which is the hallmark of maturity. This switch is perhaps most challenging in relation to our parents, from whom we can't help forever expecting certain protections and ministrations.

Nobody in the world welcomes us quite like our parents do. The reception, if we're lucky, is a simultaneous cosseting and taking for granted. An experience that's, at best, comforting and exasperating in equal measure, unique in its loaded history of give and take, its private parameters of permission and expectation. Mothers, of course, host us as no one else can – in their bodies. A nine-month gestation. Guest-ation?

'THAT'S NOT ENOUGH!' I stare into the brimming pot of kadhi, a creamy curry made with gram flour and yoghurt.

My mother ignores me, goes on stirring the turmeric-tinged sauce.

'I could eat that all on my own – for breakfast!' I'm aghast at the prospect of running short of one of my favourite dishes in the world. Give me a ladleful of this atop a mound of freshly boiled rice and I will take it whatever the hour, over whatever else is on offer. There have been times when I've eaten kadhi at every meal for days on end. Why on earth has my mother made so little?

'Eyes bigger than stomach,' she sighs.

Her words are the oldest censure of my eating life, the most frequent, and the most unheeded. They have little to do with the size of my body, which is slender, and everything to do with the size of my desire, which is vast, unwieldy, panoptic. Mum plunges the wooden spoon deep into the pot for a last stir. The paddle emerges coated with translucent slivers of onion, specks of tomato, a scattering of coriander leaves. My mouth waters, all reason drowns. I start scheming strategies to control how much might be eaten by our imminent guests. We have to use the small bowls to serve. And Mum shouldn't insist on extra helpings. And whatever happens, she can't offer anybody a portion to take home.

'Stop being so silly,' Mum says. 'There's plenty here. And anyhow, I can always make more for you.'

But it doesn't matter how much she cooks. She can never make enough. Not for me.

Mine is perhaps an odd strain of a common affliction, a variant of the consumption epidemic ravaging our capitalist societies: those of us who have the most still want more, much more, than we need. Could it be otherwise in a system premised on the false conviction that our existence as we know it depends on the continuity of one thing alone: economic growth? Our appetites must keep increasing to propel the economy. *Eyes bigger than stomach* — the refrain that sums me up also epitomises our contemporary condition. But are there situations where greed, if not excusable, is understandable, and maybe even necessary?

Kadhi is what awaits me every time I go see my mother. Mostly in London, but wherever she happens to be – Australia or Kenya, the countries where my siblings live – whenever I come, kadhi is cooked. It is what I take away from each visit as well; my mother prepares and freezes batches of the tarka, the spicy tomato base at the heart of much North Indian cuisine, the most time-consuming aspect of the dish. Roasting spices, browning onions, reducing tomatoes – this alone can take up to an hour, before the main ingredients of the dish are added and the whole mixture cooked further. In the case of kadhi, the tarka is a mix of whole fenugreek and mustard seeds, ground cumin and coriander, curry leaves, onion, garlic, turmeric, green chilli and tinned tomato. All I have to do at home in Berlin is heat up Mum's tarka, add yoghurt and flour, sprinkle fresh coriander to finish, and I have the taste of another home, the feeling of time turning in slow, savoury spirals. Each bite holds the flavour of the past and the present, a lifetime of my mother's love, her unstinting hospitality.

Things my mother has long done for me almost effortlessly become, with age and illness, more burdensome for her. This has not curbed her generosity, but every gesture costs her more. I suspect I began to notice the change long after it had started to happen. One day I went home and there was no kadhi. Mum was all apology. She had bought the ingredients, but had simply not felt up to cooking. 'But I'll do it now!' she said quickly. No doubt my face had betrayed my disappointment, which was not just about the setback to my stomach – substantial though that was – but the letdown of love. I knew that my mother would do anything for me, and the fact that she had not managed this relatively small task pained me. If even her boundless adoration, always ready to express itself, had not succeeded in pushing her over the threshold of limitation, she must be really unwell or really old. I felt her mortality, a frightening chill. She had never seemed so fragile, not even lying in a hospital bed, not even when she was totally grey from depression. I felt tremendously sorry for her – but also for myself. And I became angry, because my sense of what was most dependable in the world had been shaken. 'It won't take long.' Mum set a pan on the hob, started rifling for ingredients. I protested, both earnestly and falsely, that it wasn't necessary, I could wait, kadhi didn't matter. 'If you help me with the chopping we'll be done before you know it.' The sound of her voice was accompanied by the static of mustard seeds popping in hot oil, releasing a smell that pierced my nose as sharply as the tears welling in my eyes. 'It's the onions,' I insisted to Mum when she noticed. It was not the onions. It was life, tipping the scales of give and take.

THE WAY WE COOK for and eat with others is one of the more tangible, quotidian ways of measuring generosity. The type and amount of food offered, how it's served and to whom – these things define hospitality at the table, and beyond. Around the world, more people may be spending less time cooking – in the UK, US and Germany right now it's between five and six hours a week – and eating. In my family the ratio of food–time to life–time remains high, though, of course, we consider such a distinction spurious, because for us food is one of the most intense ways of living. We visit supermarkets as others do art galleries. We cook as others run marathons. We offer, at one spread, flavours of a number and variety that others might only encounter in a packet of pick 'n' mix.

Our family line of food fanatics may well stretch back over generations: the greed-gene honed over eons, mutated to fixate on the gratifications of grub at the expense of everything else. However, for me, it all begins with my maternal grandmother, an ardent eater, force-feeder and devout believer in the stomach as the only way to the heart: Mumji almost everybody calls her, the motherly moniker perhaps partly an acknowledgement of her role as arch-feeder. Her cooking swells sympathies and bellies, raises tempers and temperatures, sends some running and brings others back begging for more. She wields ingredients like weapons and has made food the front line in a fight for first place in the affections of the family. At her hob or her table, hospitality often holds hands with its brother word *hostility*. Both are birthed from *ghos-ti*, their ancient Indo-European root, which meant host, guest and stranger – the trio of roles through which we shift all our lives. So apt that this inescapable flux was once contained in a single word.

FOOD HAS LONG BEEN wielded as a form of power, a potent means of commending or condemning, of flaunting extravagance and displaying largesse. Ancient Roman history is replete with tales of excess, feasts as the stage for vanity and vengeance, like the notorious Emperor Elagabalus whose legendary spreads were spiked with sadistic surprises: at the end of a lavish meal that might include nightingale tongues, parrot heads and peacock brains you could be escorted to a guestroom for the night, only to find a tiger inside ready to devour you.

Every century and every territory has its fables of exorbitance: the Manchu Han Imperial Feast hosted by Kangxi, the fourth emperor of the Qing Dynasty, where 108 courses were served to more than 2,500 guests. The hundred-dish spreads laid out regularly at the behest of the Mughal Emperor Akbar. The fifty-course banquet that marked the wedding of Marie de' Medici to Henry IV, King of France, in Florence at the turn of the seventeenth century. The

night in 1817 when the future George IV of England held
a dinner in honour of the visiting Grand Duke Nicholas
of Russia, where 127 dishes, prepared by Marie-Antoine
Carême – then the greatest and most expensive chef in the
world – were served. The eighteen tonnes of food flown
to Persepolis in 1971 for a three-day celebration, apparently
'the most expensive party ever', held by the Shah of Iran
to mark his country's 2,500th anniversary. Such occasions
hint that excessive hospitality can be a form of hidden
hostility: feasting as a friendly warning of the host's means
and power.

While some have been subjected to extravagance, food
has also always been punitively withheld from others, sometimes on an enormous scale and with horrific consequences.
Since grain became a free-market commodity in the nineteenth century, profit has often been prioritised over
humanitarian protection. In his book *Late Victorian Holocausts*,
the historian Mike Davis describes the extreme weather
fluctuations in the last quarter of the nineteenth century
that led to severe drought and monsoons in parts of the
global south, including China, Brazil, Egypt and India.
Davis shows how colonial administrations exploited these
natural disasters to trigger and exacerbate famines that led
to mass deaths, which weakened the affected lands and
therefore strengthened foreign control.

When drought hit the Deccan Plateau in 1876 there was
actually a net surplus of rice and wheat in India. Yet the

viceroy, Lord Lytton, head of the British colonial admin-
istration in India, insisted the surplus be sent to England.
Almost simultaneously, Lytton was planning a spectacular
Imperial Assemblage in Delhi to proclaim Queen Victoria
Empress of India. Its climax, Davis writes, 'included a
week-long feast for 68,000 officials, satraps and maha-
rajas, the most colossal and expensive meal in world
history'. During the course of that week, Davis adds, an
estimated 100,000 Indians starved to death in Madras and
Mysore. At the height of the Indian famine, grain merchants
exported a record 6.4 million hundredweight (320,000
tonnes) of wheat. Peasants starved, but government officials
were directed 'to discourage relief works in every possible
way'. Davis's book exposes Western imperialism at its most
deliberately inhospitable: destroying people by keeping
their own food stocks from them. Suffering colonised
subjects were treated not like enemies or strangers, but as
if they were not human. By 1902, between 12 and 29
million Indians had died as a result of British policies in
the face of famine.

Power often asserts itself through excesses of both
hostility and hospitality.

I IMAGINE MUMJI FIRST truly understood the power of
food in her own small way after she used it to save her

future husband's life. Soon after their betrothal in India, in the summer of 1947, my grandfather, Papaji, got caught in the brutal upheavals of Partition. He had travelled from Amritsar to Lahore, intending to head on from there to the village of Gujranwala, where he'd been born and where his family had lived before migrating to Kenya in the 1930s. The borders arbitrarily drawn up by the British as they withdrew from India in 1947 left Gujranwala part of a new country called Pakistan. Papaji became one of the millions displaced by the chaos that accompanied the division of India – considered predominantly Hindu – to create Pakistan – conceived from the outset as an Islamic republic. This led to splits along ethnic lines across the whole subcontinent. The announcement of the new borders on 17 August, two days after the declaration of independence, triggered a mass movement of people who, fearful of what the change might mean, sought the supposed security of being amongst their own kind: Muslims in India headed to Pakistan, while Hindus and Sikhs in the territory that had become Pakistan left for India. Around 15 million people were uprooted. Communal violence erupted between all groups and up to a million died either in the fighting or from one of the diseases that were rife in the hundreds of refugee camps at which so many ended up. Papaji was stuck in one such camp for several weeks and caught typhoid. Eventually he managed to travel, with the help of a relative, back to Mumji's family home in Amritsar. He arrived utterly wasted, hardly able to walk. She had to save him. He was her only chance to escape an existence marred by a youthful mistake: a brief love affair that had ended in pregnancy and an illegitimate child. Papaji, having come from abroad, knew none of this — yet. She needed him to get well so she could get away. And so she cooked.

She painstakingly prepared all the most restorative foods, like khichari, the classic Indian comfort food, a one-pot meal of rice and lentils cooked for the ill with almost no spices so it's easier to digest. Mumji laced hers with fat dollops of butter to help Papaji gain weight faster. Soon she had him on panjiri, a delectable crumble of wheat flour, nuts and spices browned in ghee, traditionally given to nursing mothers as a nutritional supplement. Spoonful by spoonful she restored him to health. Months later, when he was fine again, they were married and travelled together to Kenya. There, Mumji often told the story of how she had saved Papaji, but other rumours were already circulating about who had really saved whom. So many hearts to win, so many tongues to still! How would Mumji manage? As with many women of her background and era, her means were limited. Food was one force she could harness, and so the kitchen became her combat zone. She would destroy any doubts about her past by cooking up a most flavoursome present.

IN ENGLISH *TO COOK something up* means to prepare food, but also to invent stories or schemes, to concoct something out of fantasy. When I first started writing I also baked a lot, mostly on days when the writing wasn't going well. It soothed me, alongside the slow and intangible creation of a novel, to cook up something that was quickly ready and edible. A cake can bring simple, instant self-gratification and appreciation from others, whereas writing – for all its rewards – is always accompanied by self-doubt. Moreover, the reactions of others, even when positive, are rarely enough for me. I'm perpetually hungry for some extra validation, which nobody in the world can give. Only in the act of writing is that hunger satisfied, for I become, briefly, bigger than myself, capable of hosting the entire universe and yet treating every single person in it as if they were my only guest. This feat feeds and sates my ravenous self, my need to be and to have everything.

Stories enact a form of mutual hospitality. What is story if not an enticement to stay? You're invited in, but right away you must reciprocate and host the story back, through concentration: whether you read or hear a narrative – from a book or a person – you need to listen to really under-stand. Granting complete attention is like giving a silent ovation. Story and listener open, unfold into and harbour each other.

A RECIPE IS A story that can't be plagiarised. Compare cookbooks by cuisine and you'll find recipes that are almost identical, distinguished by minor variations of ingredient quantity or slight deviations in procedure. Debts are gladly acknowledged, sometimes in the name – 'Julia's Apple Tart' – or in a sub-line – 'Adapted from Yotam Ottolenghi'. Recipes represent one of the easiest, most generous forms of exchange between people and cultures, especially nowadays, with online food blogs abounding and all kinds of once-exotic ingredients available at your local supermarket. Recipes are the original open source, offering building blocks that may be adjusted across time, place and seasons to create infinite dishes. You only need to successfully make a recipe once to feel it is your own. Make it three more times and suddenly it's tradition.

No wonder different societies claim the same food as their definitive, national dish. Hummus in the Middle East may well be the most contested case in point. Fed up of the endless, inconclusive debates about the true origins of this popular chickpea dip, a group of Lebanese hummus-aficionados decided to settle the matter once and for all by setting the record for making the largest tub of hummus ever in the hope that the feat would irrevocably associate hummus with Lebanon above all. The idea of consolidating their ur-hummus credentials by producing such an excess is fitting in the context of the famously profuse Arab hospitality, summed up in the half-joking warning to guests: you'll need to fast for two days before and two days after eating in an Arab household. A year after the Lebanese set their hummus record, the title was taken by a group in Israel who filled a satellite dish with four tonnes of the dip. Months later the Lebanese managed to top that and reclaim the Guinness World Record title. The dispute continues, a mild incarnation of the greater, more intractable regional conflict. I should probably refrain from dipping my finger into such loaded contests about the humble chickpea, but I adore hummus, and my favourite version is one made by a Palestinian friend – without a trace of garlic. And, of course, she is certain hummus was invented in her village.

IN THE EXTENDED FAMILY household in Nairobi where Mumji lived with Papaji during the first years of marriage, there was culinary competition of a very different sort. Food was complimented as people never could be. Papaji's family were a reticent bunch. Their approval, if it came at all, took the form of a cheeky pinch or punch. Fortunately, appreciation of edibles did not need to be expressed in words, it could be conveyed in sighs of satisfaction and second helpings and – from the ladies – sidelong requests for recipes. The latter were never obliged: Mumji evolved a repertoire of tactics for rebuffing them. 'Forget the recipe!

I'll just make it for you again,' she promised her preferred people, while those she liked less, but dared not risk alienating were told, 'There is no recipe, you just have to watch me make it.' Needless to say, the occasion would never arise. Even in the communal family kitchen she contrived to guard her methods from her in-laws. If she was ever cornered into explaining how to make a dish, she deliberately left out key ingredients or crucial steps. Even – especially – with her own daughter, my mother. Recently Mum asked Mumji to show her how to make gulab jamuns – small, deep-fried balls of milk solids soaked in sugar syrup. 'You can buy the ready mix at the Indian shop,' Mumji said. 'Have you ever done that?' Mum wondered. 'Of course not!' Mumji replied, and changed the subject.

There's someone else in our family who can't share recipes – Mumji's youngest son, an exceptional cook in his own right. The difference is, he'll do his best to tell you, but he's so inventive he can barely keep up with himself. He's one of those people who can rustle up a magical meal from the most mundane ingredients, all without planning ahead or consulting a cookbook. When he founded Foodloom, a catering company he ran with my mother in the early 2000s, they carefully noted details for every signature dish they developed together and still no recipe was ever definitive. However perfect it seemed to us, my uncle had another idea for how it might be improved. I spent periods working for the company while writing my first novel. Whatever job I was assigned, I felt my ultimate duty was simply to eat that exquisite food. I was the kitchen assistant who licks the smidgen of sauce left in the pan, the waitress who gobbles the last samosa on the tray.

Mumji, amazingly, has never even owned a cookbook, which might also account for her caginess about recipes. Alongside her reluctance to share details of her dishes, she is averse to any assistance with making them. Even now, in her late eighties, she doesn't want help in the kitchen. This is not simply down to control-freak tendencies and a fierce habit of independence. It's because she needs to commandeer any praise that the food will elicit. Every compliment and thank you has to be hers. All of it. Every last word, every sigh, every burp. All hers. Only hers. And there's never, ever enough.

'She's an amazing cook,' friends and family say about Mumji, before grudgingly adding, 'but she never shares a recipe.' Perhaps for this reason, Mumji has no really close friends. It's probably also why she finds it hard to ask for recipes. Instead, she eats with sharp attentiveness, turning food over with her fingers, scanning, sniffing and sucking in search of spice traces. Sometimes, she delves deeper with seemingly casual questions: 'Some people put ajwain in everything because it's good for digestion – what do you think?' Afterwards, she'll remark to us how disappointing the dishes were: 'Jassi has no idea about what flavours go

together! Who puts sweetcorn with fish?' Or, 'John really
fancies himself a chef, but he doesn't have a clue! Did you
see the number of cloves in that chicken?' Soon, if not
the very next day, the family might be treated to a variation
on a dish recently tasted somewhere . . . at Jassi's or John's?

You can feast on Mumji's food, but rarely do you get
to do so with her. The first time my husband dined at her
table – an invitation that finally came more than a year
after we'd met – he followed the example set by the rest
of us and filled his plate from the spread laid out for his
welcome. But when we started tucking in, he waited. 'What
about Mumji?' He pointed to the empty chair. 'She's not
coming yet,' I told him. 'Just start,' the others said. Still
he hesitated, disabled by a decorum that dictated you don't
begin eating until everyone is seated and served. A few
minutes later, Mumji entered the dining room bearing a
fresh batch of chapatis. Apron sprayed with flour, cheeks
red from heat, she went around offering the rotis, but
stopped short at the sight of my husband's untouched food.
'Eat!' she ordered. And when he tried to explain she cut
him off: 'I'm working hard so you getting everything hot
hot hot, and you letting everything go all cold. Eat!' He
obeyed and, ever after, reluctantly accepted her peculiar
protocol.

Part of Mumji's purpose in serving is to survey how
much people are ingesting. She keeps a mental tab on the
amount of helpings taken, the bowls of dhal re-filled, the

number of rotis eaten. She remembers how much you had last time and is upset if you don't outdo yourself at each subsequent meal. When my brother and cousins were teenagers they could easily consume many rotis apiece. Mumji would gloat and report, as if some world record had been broken: 'He dupped eleven!' There is a special word for it because, of course, nobody just eats her food, they dupp as if it were their last meal on earth.

Dupp, a slangy Punjabi sound, which I like to believe Mumji invented. To dupp is to eat with abandon and to excess. It's a wonderful, reckless activity that often comes with the high price tag of remorse and indigestion. This does not deter dedicated duppers. Nowadays each boy, as Mumji still calls them though all are grown men, might manage six rotis – a healthy appetite by any standards, but Mumji, still nostalgic for the heyday of dupping, continues to roll out dozens of flatbreads. They puff up on her small cast-iron thava to sighs of disappointment and mutterings about how these days everyone is on a diet. She cooks for the moments when someone's appetite will breach the quotidian limits of consumption and she can rejoice.

In contrast – possibly even in reaction – to this, my uncle's philosophy at Foodloom was leave them wanting more. This didn't mean guests were underfed, simply served enough – an aberration in a family for whom eating meant being stuffed, almost suffocating from surfeit.

Descending from such a tribe, it's no surprise that for

a long time food for me equalled going overboard: over-buying, over-catering, over-eating. Change came slowly, through a mix of choice and chance. Truth be told, mostly I've been coerced into having less by circumstance — periods of lower income, spells of illness. But that covetous core, *eyes bigger than stomach*, the part of me where greed always trumps need, remains alive and well, and constantly craving.

BEING ASKED HOW YOU made something is the ultimate compliment for most cooks. Recipes passed on this way have extra layers of flavour even before they're cooked, for they come marinated in the memory of previous incarnations.

Recipes can be both conduits of continuity and channels of change. Stuck to, modified, lost, recovered . . . recipes are records — fragile, enduring — of individual or national defeats and conquests. In this sense, little is strictly 'authentic': everything is influenced by someone or somewhere else. This is true for food, and for culture as a whole. The quest for authenticity is often more of a crusade for authority, an attempt to exclude, single out and thus narrow things down — the very opposite of hospitality.

Food was amongst the first commodities to be traded globally and this led to many cultures adopting foods that originated thousands of miles away. I always thought of chillies and coriander as quintessentially Asian ingredients. Only recently, eating dishes rich in both cooked by Brazilian friends, did I learn that they arrived in Asia in the sixteenth century with Portuguese explorers, who'd encountered them in Latin America. Before that Asian cuisine used white or black pepper to add spicy heat. Chilli was substituted because it was easier to grow and therefore cheaper.

The history of food is the history of globalisation. Every ingredient, however genuinely local it might seem, has behind – and, likely, ahead – of it a trail of travel and transformation. Still, we can't help but cling to a dream of original provenance. The very name of a dish can affect our appreciation of it. 'Give it an ethnic label,' says experimental psychologist Charles Spence, 'such as an Italian name, and people will rate the food as more authentic.'

WHEN I WAS SMALL, if my parents even casually mentioned the possibility of another sibling, I threatened to run away should it ever come to pass. I couldn't express it as such, but I felt there was no room for anyone else in our household, that there wouldn't be 'enough'. What exactly I'd be deprived of I couldn't have said. Our unit of four was privileged in many ways, my sister and I did not lack for anything, certainly not materially. Yet insecurity pervaded my childhood.

Inequality was rife in the Kenya of the 1970s and '80s in which I grew up. There was a chasm not just between rich and poor, but between black and non-black. The country had achieved independence from the British in 1963, yet remained steeped in vestiges of colonialism, not least a sordid legacy of racial hierarchy. Social interactions between different coloured people were limited. The well-off Indian community, which my family was part of, kept mostly to itself. Such exclusiveness could not spare anyone the wider reality: it was there in the shanties you passed on the way to and from your fenced-off mansion. In the young faces you turned away from when they approached your car at the traffic lights, empty palms outstretched at your window. It was there in the risk – actual, but also imagined and exaggerated – of being robbed that led to a vigil of locked doors, changing guards and perpetual suspicion. It was there in qualms about the sun, which could quickly darken your skin, and thus, it seemed, your value. Everybody around me wanted to be paler, because white people were considered better, even if they too were despised for their 'loose' ways and the power they'd lorded over us in former days. Small wonder then that fear dominated my youth. It was like a tinnitus, an indistinct buzz – sometimes loud, sometimes low, always present. A symptom, I would understand only much later, of sensing injustice but not being equipped to confront it, let alone try to do anything about it.

Yet there were instants when the differences and their attendant anxieties dissolved. It happened when your nanny ate fat slices of homemade pizza with you while your parents went out to a party. When you bought corn on the cob from a street vendor and each yellow kernel, roasted brown and infused with charcoal fumes, tasted mildly smoked, and afterwards the scent lingering on your fingers was the smell of the evening near a shanty town as hundreds of jikos were stoked into action to heat up hundreds of dinners. When the ice-cream seller rang his bell and kids from all over would gather round his cart clamouring for a Red Devil. The lollies would stain your mouth, tongue and teeth, so that for hours after eating every one of you, whoever you were, resembled a vampire freshly feasted on blood. It happened at inter-school tournaments, where there was an almost democratic mingling when someone passed around a pack of Mabuyu, candied baobab seeds. The pinky-purple candy, possibly the cheapest, commonest confection in Kenya, came in clear, unbranded little plastic bags, with no hint of an ingredients list to betray the vast quantity of sugar required to make the salty-sweet nuggets that furred your mouth and left you fiercely thirsty. The Marmite of Kenya: people either love or hate Mabuyu. I couldn't stand them, but ate them now and then out of a desperate wish to have something – anything – in common with everybody else.

My family's circle of friends, though all Indian, was

religiously diverse. We would regularly get together with Hindus, Muslims or other Sikhs for what the adults called 'kitty parties', where each family would bring a dish. Such events took place over all kinds of occasions, from Eid to Diwali to Vaisakhi to Christmas. Sometimes there was a karoga, the Kenyan–Indian equivalent of a barbecue, then all the dads would take centre stage for the cooking, bottles of Tusker in hand, proudly performing the hospitality that was usually the unremarked domain of women. The dads could just karoga a bit and get all the credit, while women like my mum could gain attention only through organising elaborate charity balls or preparing sumptuous dinners.

Karoga means 'to stir' in Swahili. Over the course of a few hours, a meat curry is cooked outside on a huge cast-iron thava, the pan set over a charcoal-fuelled jiko. All the ingredients – meat, onions, spices, tomatoes – are chopped and prepared in advance so that the men – it's usually just men – can hang around the thava and sip beer while slowly simmering and stirring the curry to completion. The running joke is that the more alcohol is imbibed, the better the food tastes, at least to those who have – or are – drunk.

It's said the tradition dates back to the early twentieth century when Indian workers, brought over by the British to build the Uganda Railway, started cooking their meal while on the job. They'd add different ingredients, stir each time they passed the pan, and after a few hours they'd have a fragrant lunch. A charming tale, though one that's hard to believe given the terrible conditions under which workers laboured to build the Lunatic Line, as the railway was dubbed. It's unlikely there was time for slow-cooking curries during a building process marked by all kinds of disasters, including attacks by wild animals. Four Indians died for every mile of the track, which cut across the country, from Mombasa at the coast to Lake Victoria near the border with Uganda.

Karoga is no longer the sole preserve of Kenyan Indians; it has gone mainstream. Restaurants across Nairobi are now dedicated to this ritual, which has managed to override cultural boundaries in a society still scarred by racial difference. It could be because the karoga clubs offer a situation where you are served, but still cook yourself; you pay, yet work. Without the clear dynamic of host and guest maybe everyone's skin colour matters less. The majority of establishments offer halal meat. Many Kenyans — over 80 per cent of whom are Christian — are reassured by the label, which they see as a guarantee that they won't get dog or donkey meat in disguise. Alcohol remains an essential part of the karoga experience and that may be the real key to karoga kinship.

FOOD CAN DIVIDE AS much as connect. Even where a group is relatively homogenous, difference can suddenly sizzle, like water splashed on a hot griddle. I saw this in my father's annoyance that our Muslim friends didn't eat any meat dishes at our house — because they, rightly, assumed it wasn't halal. 'That's it! We're not inviting them again!' he would rage as my mother put away excess leftovers of chicken, which the guests hadn't touched. 'Who do they think they are? I don't want to see them any more. Do you hear me? Never!' Quick to anger, my father also calmed down pretty fast. Next time we were on the way to visit Muslim friends he'd swear that he wouldn't have any meat they served — because he knew it would be halal. By the time we were around their table, his misgivings would have disappeared and he'd tuck into whatever was on offer, extending compliments and having seconds. Years later, after my family moved briefly to London, my parents themselves sometimes bought meat from a halal butcher in Tooting. What was the alternative when certain dishes, like lamb pilau or samosas, turned out much better made with the less fatty meat, which just happened to be halal?

There's nothing like desire — whatever its object — to help us forget our compunctions. Food can make some of us compulsive and thus push us past certain limits — of propriety, of decency, of sanity. Whenever this happens to me, my husband says I get 'The Look' — a tense, hunted, frenzied expression that announces greed has taken hostage all sense. Often at pains to appear polite and decent, I have consigned manners to oblivion and chased canapé trays at parties, helping myself to handfuls at a time. Normally eager to avoid the cold at all costs, I have pulled on coat and boots and headed out into the midnight snow to buy a packet of crisps. Generally disposed to honesty, I have lied that there are no leftovers only to secretly scoff them all myself. I never understood the restraint practised by believers whose faith imposed food restrictions. How could they resist?

If only my best friend tasted bacon, I was convinced she would be converted to pork regardless of her loyalty to Islam. One of my more ignoble childhood pranks involved disguising some ham in the food we served her and then trying not to gloat as she ate, exclaiming how delicious it was. Only after she'd finished did I reveal my ploy. Her utter mortification unsettled me. The taste had changed nothing; indeed, the fact that she'd liked it made her feel guiltier. I felt bad too, though that didn't stop me from trying the trick again, as if I might still tempt her out of her convictions. For long afterwards, a question puzzled me: how did ideology have the power to proscribe pleasure? Then, in my thirties, I became a vegetarian and finally grasped, in my own way, how a belief could not just curb but entirely cancel out certain cravings. The impossible happened: I could pass over food I'd once adored without a pang. If belief is a choice, keeping faith is when a choice becomes habit.

My dad may have forgotten his grudges in the face of

an aromatic lamb dish, but there were deeper differences that he could not dismiss. Some distinctions, it seems, won't be bridged, some borders won't be crossed, no matter how many meals are shared with others, no matter how many foreign delicacies are consumed. That's why, though some of their closest friends were Muslim, some of their dearest in-laws white, my parents warned that my sister and I should never become romantically attached to a Muslim, or a black person, or a white (in that order). Of course there was no logical explanation for this racist rule. The best my parents could manage was that it was against our religion.

Looking back, I think we saw ourselves as victims and therefore somehow absolved from any duty to others, however much worse their plight. On our tables there was plenty, but our minds were impoverished, our imaginations limited. We prided ourselves on our hospitality, but had little sense of just how far the act could stretch — and in the stretching, who it might enable us to become.

PERHAPS BECAUSE OF MY cravings for security and certainty, I'm no neophile when it comes to food. As a child this meant always ordering scampi and chips at the Carnivore restaurant on Sundays. Eating only the orange Smarties. Asking for my mum's devil's food cake on every birthday. I would even pester my friends to get their mothers to make things I liked if I was visiting: Aunty Sajida's mince and potato koftas, Aunty Bubbles' risotto. At the same time, I suffered from food envy: the meal of my fellow diners, or strangers' dishes on an adjoining table, would tantalise me. It was as though I wanted something else − but not on my own plate, or of my own volition. One way around this was to try, where possible, to taste everyone else's fare. 'No, you can't have a bite!' my sister would snap, on principle, whenever my fork hovered towards her dinner.

Even now, I try to avoid disappointment by sticking to what I know. It seems I'm not alone in this tendency. What else explains the persistence of vanilla as the most popular ice-cream flavour almost everywhere? Despite the proliferation of ice-cream variety and availability − from Brazil to China to New Zealand − vanilla still rules. In the UK, sandwich leader of the world, the growing array of bread types and fillings is astonishing. Combinations change by the season and the industry remains on a search for the winning combo that might join the ranks of egg mayo, bacon-lettuce-tomato aka BLT, and chicken salad − 'the core', as they're called, of the business: these three versions account for 80 per cent of all sandwich sales, though they comprise only about 20 per cent of what's on offer. Millions of British people eat the same type of sandwich every workday for the whole of their lives. Across the globe there must be millions more for whom the taste of lunch, whatever its unchanging form, is a welcome, necessary constant amidst all the change that constitutes life.

There is a special sensation to be had in tried and tested tastes, in experiencing things again and again, treating ingredients or flavours like a button through which you might pause time and still keep certain pleasures forever on replay. Yet, however doggedly you press those buttons to conjure the familiar, there always comes a point at which you're somehow, if only briefly, made to stop and switch track. For me, this usually occurs when there is no other choice, no similar option – because if a thing is gone my first impulse is to replace it immediately with something almost identical. The kind term for such a disposition is *creature of habit*, but sometimes reluctance in the face of unexpected novelty merits a harsher description: stubborn, selfish, set in your ways. All these have, justifiably, been levelled at me by loved ones and by my own internal chorus of critics. How can I be stricken by a modification to my preferred brand of espresso? How much longer can I go on lamenting that the Swiss chocolate-maker Sprüngli has discontinued its milk chocolate, cranberry and caramelised pecan bar, and that there appears to be no equivalent in the whole wide world? What sort of person angsts over such trivialities when there are far more serious issues at hand? A frivolous, entitled prig? A passionate obsessive? Whatever the colour of the charge, there's no denying the

complaint of desperation at its core. How will you deal
with big changes, my sister has often pressed me, if you
can't handle tiny ones? She doesn't understand that the
tiny ones are harder to accept precisely because they should
be easier to avert. Of course I dislike the big stuff too, but
it bulldozes right over you, leaving no chance to resist —
though not resisting doesn't mean accepting. I stupidly
seethe and suffer even when I know I can't alter a thing.

WHO ARE WE? NO society can avoid that destabilising question. It pealed shrill through our daily existence in Kenya,
vibrated in our veins and would not be stilled either by
efforts to ignore or answer it. How narrowly that 'we' was
defined! It was usually our Sikh family, occasionally our
Indian community, and sometimes, at its widest, it was
our British citizenship, with the associated personal advan-
tages and aspirations. Bizarrely, this equation of identity,
though built from the variables of history, politics and
economy, did not consciously consider them. No wonder
that we struggled to work out our place in the world.
Without any comprehensive knowledge of the past we
couldn't even begin to add up our myriad connections to
others across space and time, couldn't figure out that we
were more than the sum of our most obvious parts. We
were caught in a strange bind, us British Indians in Kenya:

colonised twice over, materially the better off for it, but completely confused mentally about who we were, and therefore where we really belonged and what we owed.

Deciding what exactly is on your plate is one of the few seemingly autonomous choices some of us can make – and it's certainly easier to control than what goes on beyond your gate. The edge of the plate is like a border emphasising the specificity of a choice, the relations, traditions and dispositions that influence it. What we eat enters our bodies and becomes part of us in an intimate way. Food forms and reveals us. This is why discussions about it can get so heated.

In defending a sausage some Germans claim to be upholding a whole culture. In fact, they are protecting their own preferences, their own sense of what's superior, of how life should taste. At first I was contemptuous when a public debate flared about the appropriateness – or not – of serving pork in German schools where there are large numbers of Muslim children. This particular discussion took place in 2016, a year after around 800,000 mainly Syrian refugees, fleeing war in their country, had arrived in Germany. Why don't they just introduce vegetarian meals and be done with it? I wondered, irritated by the brigade that acts as though identity is encased in a *Wurst*. I felt a bit more sympathetic when I considered that the food fights were merely ersatz battles for clashes on more profound questions: *Who are we becoming? Who do we want to be?*

Can the answer lie in a sausage? Perhaps only in so far as one never exactly knows — or wants to! — all the contents within the casing. Identity too is a mince of sorts: besides the meat of family and country that forms its most obvious substance, a lot of foreign stuff (though perhaps not recognised as such) spices it up. It's bulked by a sprawl of stories that can barely be contained, and imbued with the flavour of history, which — always present, whether or not you know it — stealthily seasons the self.

'NOW DON'T START EATING like you've been starved all your life!' my mother would warn whenever we were en route to someone's house. The co-founder of Lady Chic, a finishing school in Nairobi, Mum was a stickler for etiquette. My sister and I were trained early in the 'proper' ways to sit at the table, to hold cutlery, to ask for seconds. Much to Mum's chagrin, all this grooming could fly out the window the moment I encountered any temptation.

Food at other people's homes has always held an irresistible appeal for me. Even the most ordinary ingredients assume an aura of novelty from being presented in a different setting. There's also the jittery excitement — especially with my same-again tendency — of being subject to someone else's preferences and maybe forced to try something new. As a guest, it's hard to refuse — at least without being rude – your host's offerings. The role of guest comes with some burdens, but being a good guest can bring unexpected gifts. The first taste of a thinly shaved fennel salad served by a friend set off my love affair with this vegetable: for months I had it regularly – raw, roasted, braised. The same has happened with rhubarb, with miso, with ricotta, pumpkin seed oil, za'atar.

Dora pagya is Mumji's Punjabi expression for such food crushes. The phrase suggests a kind of attack that exerts a fever-like grip. The fever usually breaks only when I've overdosed on the flavour of the moment. But afterwards the ingredient remains part of my food universe, orbiting just outside the field of appetite until it is once again pulled into the centre of craving. Perhaps the initial gorging is a way of taming strange new tastes, subjugating them by sheer force of repetition into familiarity, into the realm of the known and the safe. I do this with ideas too, binge-reading certain writers, devouring and digesting their thoughts until they fuse with and fuel my own.

If only the same were possible with people! Some form of incorporeal cannibalism that enabled you to ingest others, leaving each person entirely intact and inviolate, yet completely understood. Romantic love offers a version of this, but that all-consuming, abiding mutual regard is rare, something which, if you're lucky, you get to have with just one person in a lifetime. Literature, more than any other art form, can give you this visceral knowledge of a stranger, but the experience — whether through writing or reading — is so solitary, so personal. Theatre, cinema or concerts can foster an atmosphere where a crowd simultaneously opens up to something new, but for most people such events are the exception. Maybe food really is the simplest way for people anywhere to share with each other. Eating is the one universal, daily activity that underpins human life. However much or little we think about it, food is a force — and when shared its power may be amplified.

OF THE MORE THAN 15,000 initiatives started in Germany since 2015 to help arriving refugees, a significant proportion have been based around cooking and eating together as a step towards fostering community. Many of the gatherings seek to unite long-time local residents with the newly arrived, to introduce strangers who may not even have a language in common. They meet in neutral spaces, such as youth clubs, school halls or sports centres, where all can be both host and guest, contributing however they feel able: chopping vegetables, playing music or clearing up.

Early in 2016, I was invited by a friend to join one of the monthly gatherings that she, as a member of the Klausenerplatz Refugee Initiative, helps organise at the Stadtteilzentrum Charlottenburg in Berlin. Hers is one of many such *Vereine*, or associations, which exemplify German civil society. There are over 600,000 *Vereine* in Germany – every second citizen is a member of one, which accounts for the joke that if three Germans meet they found a club. Around 24 per cent of the *Vereine* are focused mainly on assisting migrants or refugees. Whatever their purpose – culture, sport, social integration – *Vereine* are registered as charities. They are led by volunteers and financed mostly through private donations, though some also qualify for state funding – the Klausenerplatz Initiative is one of these. This neighbourhood group works to help newcomers feel at home through get-togethers and language courses. It was set up in 1999, but was never busier than in 2016. On the day I went, I sat at a table with Syrians, Afghans, Iraqis and Germans, at least four mother tongues between ten of us, and only two people capable of translating a tiny fraction of all that was waiting to be asked or said. At the surrounding tables too, more people seemed to be looking or nodding at each other than talking. I was glad to be there, yet a little frustrated by the limited exchange. I was also having weird pangs – not of hunger exactly, at least not hunger for food. It took a while to recognise the old childhood throb of insecurity, the craving for certainty. I felt odd because, fifteen years after I'd started living in Germany, I was, for the first time, aware of not being in the minority: there were way more brown than white faces in the room. I blended, on the surface at least, into this throng of displaced persons as I never had in any other public space of this city. Yet, at that moment, I did not feel particularly at home. Quite the opposite, I felt like the outsider, awkward and with no clear purpose or role. Then my friend came and took me on a tour of the place.

In the kitchen, a dozen-odd helpers were preparing a feast, collaborating through hand gestures and intuition to create specialities from Kerala, Kurdistan, Kabul. In the back rooms, musicians from all over were improvising, practising what they would soon play to entertain everyone. Children ran shouting into and out of the garden: I had no idea what they were saying, but their squeals were perfectly legible. Delight and despair sound the same everywhere. Teenage boys leant, with practised casualness, against the walls of the corridor, watching the proceedings with seeming indifference. Others wove through the tightly packed tables in the dining hall with bottles of juice and soda, topping up glasses and flashing awkward smiles at the thanks that came in different tones and hues. When the food was ready, the fragmented crowd of hundreds suddenly cohered and I was briefly part of that convergence. Words didn't matter. In sharing a meal everyone communicated through the vocabulary of victuals. They discovered bits of each other through the dictionary of dishes. They learned a new lexicon of largesse and loss, longing and laughter that could pave the way for the exchanges of the future.

That was a defining moment: the synchronous sense of otherness and likeness, the discomfort of not knowing if

I was more host or guest, and the relief of finding common ground at the table, realising the equalising potential in breaking bread as strangers.

Sometimes, I wish there were some harmless form of exposure that could reveal us all, briefly but instantly, intimately and enduringly, to one another. What hospitality might evolve from such deep, expansive understanding?

'LOVE BEGINS WHEN SOMETHING impossible is overcome,' Alain Badiou reflects. Might the same be said of hospitality? The act of accepting from another, of receiving the other — real reciprocity — only begins, only touches the rim of true hospitability, when done against the odds, almost against one's own inclination.

That imagined sibling of whom my parents had sometimes spoken, and whom I had long dreaded, finally arrived: a brother. The circle of love did not, as I had feared, shrink. On the contrary: all our hearts expanded with fresh love for him, and in him all our connections and emotions had a new point at which to meet and from which to spread. So, at the age of twelve, came my first realisation that love, at least, is not a finite reserve. Love is the ultimate natural resource, boundless, giving as it grows, growing as it gives. Decades later I would read the French writer Hélène Cixous and consider it differently:

'What we love is the undesired. The arrival of what is desired satisfies but does not fill with enthusiasm . . . More than everything in the world we love the creature we would never have expected. Never thought of loving.'

I wonder if my parents had a version of this recognition when I broke their rule about whom I could love and fell for my husband, who is white, and also — to their initial horror — German, divorced, twelve years older than me. I wonder if, after all the disappointment, argument and temporary estrangement — the year of resistance before they finally invited him to their table — they felt the frisson of embracing the foreign, the stupendous surprise of appreciating what you never knew you wanted. I wonder if whole societies can also experience such a shift. How might such a collective apprehension look and feel? Perhaps like the arrival of the first groups of refugees in Germany in the summer of 2015, when crowds of Germans welcomed the crowds of those who had fled as though they were athletes reaching the finish line of the world's most gruelling race.

MY PARENTS ARE JUST nominally Sikh. So the idea that my sister and I should keep our love interests in line with our religion rang hollow to me from the first — which is not to say that I didn't fear the threatened ostracism if the dictate wasn't followed. The heart may not follow orders, but it remembers them. Those childhood commands about who was worthy of affection – or not – were drummed in so hard they still pulse faintly in me even as my heart and mind roar their own demands. You try to unlearn prejudice beat by beat, correcting yourself each time it pulses to the fore. Still, sometimes it's there before you can stop it, tapping out its false lore, tripping you into its trap.

Parshad, traditionally made from equal parts of wholegrain wheat flour, sugar and clarified butter, is served as a blessing to all attendees at the end of every Sikh prayer service – the idea being that nobody should leave the temple empty-handed, or empty-stomached. Cooked in great batches, the hot pudding is transferred into large metal bowls, then covered with a white cloth and placed beside the Guru Granth Sahib, the Sikh holy book, for the duration of the service. There, imbued by divine verses, it slowly cools. Afterwards, a Granthi or a sewadar (a volunteer server) will dole out parshad to the congregation.

In Kenya parshad was made with fine semolina, not flour. It was the first version I knew, and therefore, evermore, the truest – never mind the edicts of the Sikh authorities in Amritsar who claimed the wheatflour sort, made to Guru Nanak's original prescription, as the only acceptable variant.

I loved the moment when a warm, golden clump imprinted with the server's fingers was dropped into my waiting palms. It was always the same: sublimely sweet and superbly comforting. That was religion for me: a mound of heaven in my hand, a taste at once chaste and decadent. I'd devour it and then, fingers slick with residues of fat, I would turn to my mum who, having taken a bite of her portion, would give the rest to me with the injunction: make sure you leave space for lunch. I nodded, always convinced that my stomach had plenty of room: there was not enough parshad in the universe to satisfy me. Not sated even after eating Mum's share, my eyes would follow the sewadar, waiting for him to finish his round – then I'd run up and ask for another helping. There were usually a couple of other kids trailing the sewadar, the greedy ones, sybarites in the making, who knew that here you could ask for more and not be told 'no'.

Stuffed with parshad I was, as my mother feared, never that keen on the langar that followed the service. The food was tasty enough, but the portions were too generous even though I pleaded – *Thora denah! Only a little!* – to stay the hand of the sewadars who stood in line behind a row of steaming pails ladling each of the day's dishes into a separate compartment of the stainless steel, tray-like plates held out by each diner. The rule, under which my sister and I daily toiled, to finish whatever was on our plates – *Think of all the starving millions!* – became stricter at the gurdwara. This was 'holy' food, after all, paid for by donations, prepared by volunteers and offered to all as a gift. So my sister and I would hunch over our meal, force down as much as we could manage and then find ways to make it look like we'd finished. A pool of dhal would be smeared across various sections of the plate, vegetables might be dropped into a metal water tumbler, leftover bits of roti could be rolled and pushed up a sleeve or into a sock. We had become practised in such tricks at home, where it was not unusual for us to hide bits of food somewhere on our person and then ask to be excused to go to the toilet, where the unwanted food would be flushed down the loo. I'm still not sure why we were such picky eaters when my mum cooked so well, served us mostly things we liked, and not too much at that. Perhaps we were just generally too well fed to get really hungry. In any case, we weren't allowed to leave the table until our plates were clean, and at the gurdwara too we waited for the glint of permission in Mum's eye before we could take our trays to the spot where they were all piled before being washed.

Today, around one-third of food produced worldwide for human consumption every year gets somehow lost or squandered. In the global south, this mostly occurs due to lack of adequate cold-storage facilities. Such limitations mean, for instance, that half of all the fruit and vegetables produced in Africa degrade soon after harvest, even before they reach market. Various initiatives are trying to address this problem, which if solved could save enough food for another 300 million people. In Western countries, well over half of the spoilage occurs in homes, restaurants and shops — mostly food that isn't eaten. Every year, consumers in richer nations waste almost as much food as the entire net food production of sub-Saharan Africa.

I feel guilty about wastage, and generally try to buy less than I used to, but I still can't force myself to finish things. My own immediate 'needs' often override the practical or ethical imperative of what needs eating. I remain at the mercy of food-moods, imagining the next meal before the current is complete, planning what to buy while the fridge is still full.

MY PARENTS MUST HAVE mentioned that the langar at the temple was a communal meal open to everyone, not just Sikhs. Yet the significance of this didn't register for me until my grandfather, Papaji, explained it.

'Anyone can come and share in the langar,' he told me, when I was nine or ten. 'Langar means "community kitchen", and anybody can join the community.'

I was stunned. 'Anyone?' I repeated, wondering if that included black people, since I had never eaten with anyone black apart from our servants in Nairobi. With white people it was a little different because, though my parents had no white friends, we did have some white in-laws and I had a few white schoolmates. There was only one black boy in my class and hardly any black students at my school.

'Absolutely anybody,' Papaji said. 'You don't have to be invited, you can just show up and you will be gladly received.'

The practice of offering a free meal to which all are welcome was part of Sikhism from its inception in the fifteenth century. The langar, implemented by the founder, Guru Nanak, was a way of expressing two central tenets: equality between all human beings and service to the community. A meal was prepared and served by volunteers, and all those who wished to partake of it sat down on the floor together to eat. The idea that anyone could help cook the food and anyone could consume it was especially radical in India, where for centuries caste distinctions manifested most obviously around food. In Hinduism especially, there were, and remain, taboos against eating with – and sometimes even eating anything touched by – those outside one's caste group, of lower caste, or of a different religion. The Sikh langar is vegetarian so as not to offend other religious sensibilities. Sitting together was a way to bring everyone to the same level regardless of rank, class, gender or denomination. Across the world, including at the Golden Temple in Amritsar – the Sikh's holiest site – some gurdwaras still follow the original custom of eating seated on the floor. And across the world Sikh temples still maintain that everyone has an open invitation to the langar.

IN A DIALOGUE ABOUT hospitality between the French writer Hélène Cixous and the philosopher Jacques Derrida, the latter acknowledged that 'unconditional hospitality is impossible'. Yet, he went on, 'the only possibility of the thing is the experience of the impossibility'.

When I first came upon the notion of unconditional hospitality I experienced a kind of vertigo – similar to the sensation I'd had as Papaji explained the langar, but more intense and destabilising. What was Derrida suggesting?

> Absolute hospitality requires that I open up my home and that I give not only to the foreigner (provided with a family name, with the social status of being a foreigner, etc.), but to the absolute, unknown, anonymous other, and that I *give place* to them, that I let them come, that I let them arrive, and take place in the place I offer them, without asking of them either reciprocity (entering in a pact) or even their names.

Outrageous, fabulous, preposterous! However, the more I thought about it, the more reasonable this premise appeared – and not because it started to seem more realistic. On the contrary, it felt ever more manifestly unrealistic. Yet the very unattainability makes it exemplary as a goal. It continually flabbergasts you and thus demands a constant vigilance of yourself – your inclinations and prejudices, assumptions and actions. This doesn't mean slipping into moral or cultural relativism, but maintaining an ever-receptive stance.

'If I know what to decide, there is no more responsibility to take,' Derrida said. The onus on us, he implies, is to open up again and again. To take, in every instance where instinct bids retreat and refusal, one more step towards the horizon of unconditional hospitality. This attitude – or at least the effort to cultivate it – could be a kind of compass. The needle doesn't necessarily orient you in any one direction. It spins, dizzyingly, suggesting a myriad ways, all of them beyond you, all beckoning: try me and see.

What opportunities do we get to extend unconditional hospitality? It's offered mostly where there is some kind of involuntary dependency: to babies, the very ill, very elderly and to the very unfortunate. Otherwise, most healthy relations – whether personal or official – are conditional, based on privately or publically set rules of reciprocity. Those who disregard these tend to be regarded at best as rebellious, more typically as perverse or criminal, even as freaks. We're suspicious not only of those who take, but also those who give too much. Criticism is implicit in the words we have for such people: scroungers or do-gooders.

Charity begins at home. The old proverb suggests we must care for those close to us before helping those further away. *Charity* originally denoted love for fellow human beings, later it assumed the philanthropic associations of giving material or financial assistance to the less well off. It's fitting that love is at the root of charity, for to love is to be in a state of munificence, more receptive to receiving and bequeathing. Love is essentially an impulse towards giving unconditionally. It is in love – with partners, family, friends – that we most regularly, if fleetingly, scale the heights of unconditionality.

Our first training in loving, thus in giving and taking, happens in the sphere of family. At a certain stage, the sense of obligation, the impulse towards donation, extends beyond those we know towards those we wish to know better. For some, the circle of responsibility expands even further to include those who are not known and never will be, but towards whom, it's understood, there is nevertheless a kind of duty, a contract called humanity, an ideal of universal love, which binds every individual to all others. For some, the circle grows even wider, to include the earth and everything that lives on it.

Until my late twenties, I didn't consider that I might owe anything to anyone outside the ring of close acquaintance. In Kenya everybody I knew had shied away from such considerations and my apolitical education in the UK didn't touch on them either. When I was nineteen my father went bankrupt and my family was forced to leave Kenya. It seemed like the worst thing that could have happened. In retrospect, it was the best: it shook us all, to differing degrees, out of the complacency of privilege.

But even this fall was somewhat cushioned because we had the security of British citizenship and a welfare state to rely on. My sister and I were entitled to a free university education, my mother and brother were eligible for a council flat. Moreover, we had family in the UK who were able to help us. Even in adversity we were better off than most of the black Kenyans we had left behind. Still, our straitened circumstances confirmed my impression that nobody counted as much as my nearest and dearest – and it was demanding enough to help them. I may well have stuck with that view much longer had I not read Peter Singer's *The Life You Can Save*.

In his book, Peter Singer challenges us to think about what it takes to live ethically in a world where millions die unnecessarily each year or are trapped in extreme poverty. Around the world, he points out, a billion people struggle to live each day on less than many of us pay for bottled water that we don't even need. He proposes The Pledge – a public standard, with a minimum of 1 per cent of income, for what we should donate to charity. The Pledge involves signing up to this goal to give more. Within hours of finishing the book, I took The Pledge, set up direct debits to different charities and resolved to give more to help the world's poor.

I had occasionally given to charity before, but usually in one-off responses to appeals after certain catastrophes. I felt I wasn't obliged to help others since my immediate family members were now less well off than they had been. *The Life You Can Save* helped me see how even those who are poor in the West are often better off than the poor in the developing world.

I wrote a letter to Peter Singer, describing how when I started giving I realised that I have more than I need, and I'm actually able to give more than I had imagined. I don't miss the money that I give. If it hadn't gone to charity I would probably have spent it on buying things I didn't need.

Peter himself donates a third of his income to what he calls 'effective' charities – organisations that are rigorously evaluated on their efficacy. He's part of a social and philo-sophical movement called Effective Altruism whose advocates use evidence and reason to find ways of giving that will be most beneficial to others. Many are 'extreme altruists' who, you might say, have a compulsion for giving: they work mainly to donate much of their salary. My 1 per cent seemed so measly in comparison yet, at the moment when I signed up, this commitment felt like a huge step.

Most people, if asked, agree that it is better to give than to receive. Science confirms that acts of giving tap into the brain's pleasure circuits, notably the mesolimbic system that usually lights up in response to delights like great food or sex. I think I'm equally thrilled by both giving and receiving. In fact, for a long time (and still, more often than I like) I gave in the hope of getting something back

— which may well be the worst reason since such acts, perhaps rightly, are rarely (in the giver's eyes) adequately requited.

'To do something,' Derrida said, 'it is necessary to do more than what one can do.'

Peter Singer kindly acknowledged that first letter I sent him, and a few years later he got in touch again to ask about my giving. He was working on a new book about Effective Altruism and was curious about how much I was now donating and to which organisations. Maybe my experience could be an interesting example for his book?

I was at once flattered and mortified by his message. Since that first flurry of setting up transfers to various charities I had moved little beyond giving 1 per cent. I consoled myself that I had at least given more time to various causes, but I burned with quiet shame at how little progress I'd made on extending my Pledge. Time was precious, but back then I felt I had enough to not mind putting some of it in the service of others. Money, on the other hand, always felt short because there were so many things I wanted for myself. And so, as if exercising some sort of perverse reverse hospitality, I'd rationalised that because I was giving 1 per cent away I could spend more on myself.

In Peter's book there's a thought experiment in which you walk by a pond where several children are drowning while a few adults stand at the edge of the water. You immediately jump in and drag out one child. But there are still two in trouble and nobody else is moving to help. Do you think: 'Well, I've done my bit, now it's up to someone else?' Or do you try to save another child?

Having kids and raising them to be generous and engaged individuals is one way of upholding the social contract. Procreation is perhaps the basis for the ancient understanding of reciprocity between generations. I never felt a strong, lasting pull to have children, whereas the need to write tugs at me tenaciously. So the question arises: if I'm substituting the literary for biology, if my offspring are to be books not babies, how can I fulfil my part of the social contract? Much as I delight in words, depend on them, value them over all instruments – simply to put more words into the world didn't seem sufficient.

The idea behind The Pledge is that it's a moving target – like the horizon of unconditional hospitality. Effective Altruists focus on achieving a new 'personal best' the way athletes train to beat a personal record. As it's explained on *The Life You Can Save* website: 'rather than set goals based on comparison to other people's performance or a lofty and possibly unrealistic ideal, we use our own past performance as the measure for goal-setting. In order for a goal to improve performance, it must be both a bit of a stretch and attainable.' Unfortunately, I tend to be more motivated by the idea of beating someone else than beating myself – a tragic residue of my education at a highly competitive school in Kenya where everything from sports to poetry recital to maths prowess was measured not in pleasure or improvement, but in top marks and medals. Clearly, there was no way I could compete with the Extreme Altruists. What on earth was I going to say to Peter? Eventually, I wrote back. I told him that a few years into taking *The Life You Can Save* Pledge I'm only just beginning to grasp its essence: that Effective Altruism requires an active, evolving engagement with the world. Like all vital facets of our lives, altruism needs to be watched, challenged and nurtured; otherwise it risks becoming stale and automatic. I added that I now wanted to try and give 10 per cent of my income to charity.

Peter replied, 'I think it will be good to have someone like you in the book, to make a contrast with the more extreme EAs who donate very large portions of their income.' And so *The Most Good You Can Do* features a person called Priya Basil as an example of someone who aspires to Effective Altruism. A person I try and repeatedly fail to be, a person who is my best self and a complete stranger.

That title, it strikes me, may capture the essence of hospitality. The most good you can do. How little that takes. And how very much.

THE GURDWARA LANGAR INVITATION isn't really unconditional: on entering the temple you're required to remove your shoes and cover your head. In some more modern temples, where such rules are not strictly enforced, it's quite possible that you could get to the dining hall without following either requirement – but not in Berlin's Kögelstrasse gurdwara. I went there for the first time one Sunday while deep in writing this book and thinking about hospitality. I wanted to experience the langar again as a stranger, to see who else was there and how they were treated. I phoned beforehand and learned that the langar was served at around 2 p.m. Not wanting to look like I'd turned up just to eat, I arrived with my husband at about 1.30 prepared to sit through half an hour of the service – anticipating, of course, the added reward of parshad, which is usually only given out in the prayer hall.

I was surprised to hear a young Sikh explain in German where we could take off our shoes and leave our coats. It's absurd that this should have made any impression on me – we were in Germany after all. Nevertheless, it was disorientating because it confounded both my experience and my expectation of Sikhs speaking only Punjabi and English – or maybe Swahili, though that was so long ago the effect has faded. For my part, I seemed to forget all my German, and could only come up with responses in Punjabi or English.

Upstairs, the Darbar Sahib resembled the prayer halls in every other gurdwara I'd ever entered. The floor, padded with foam to make it easier to sit on, was covered with huge white sheets, like a giant, austere bed. A stark contrast to the elaborate pedestal on which the holy book lay, propped on pillows and draped in bright, sequined fabrics.

The size of the congregation was astonishing — up to 500 people, many of the men wearing turbans. I rarely saw Sikhs in the city, at least not in the parts I frequented. Once again, I was not in the minority: besides my husband, there were three other white people, a family of converts it appeared; the man and woman sported the five 'K's — Kesh, Kangha, Kara, Kachera, Kirpan — that Sikhs are required to wear at all times. These items help distinguish a Sikh from others in a crowd and also serve as personal reminders of commitment to the faith. The couple each wore a turban into which the Kangha, a small comb, was tucked. They both had the Kara, a thick steel bracelet, on one wrist, and wore Kachera, baggy white cotton shalwar kameez, over which a Kirpan, a sheathed dagger, hung from a belt slung around the waist. Their attire suggested they were following the religious observances more strictly than any of the others present.

I sat through the kirtan, Punjabi hymns sung by priests, thinking how such spaces, and others like it where people can gather in their preferred fashion and constellations, can operate publically with the consent of the state even if they are privately funded, and reflect a form of hospitality. Then I began to wonder what might be served for lunch. Food in the gurdwara can't be tasted until it has been blessed. The cooks and volunteers prepare every meal without even checking the seasoning. When everything is ready, a small portion of each dish is set on a platter and taken from the kitchen to the prayer hall. There it sits, like the parshad, marinating in holy verse. The platter is later taken back to the kitchen, each portion returned and mixed into its larger counterpart, the blessings stirred through the pot like a last pinch of salt. Then it's ready to serve.

At 2.15 the service was still going. I looked over at my husband, who was seated on the other side of the room with all the men. His tall, lean body was folded in three as he sat with knees bent and pulled into his chest, arms wrapped around his legs. He was ostensibly the outsider here, yet his patka — a cotton head covering, like a hand-kerchief with strings at two corners that tie at the back of the skull — hinted at some degree of belonging. Usually, visitors make do with one of the standard squares of cloth kept at gurdwaras. My husband's black patka was distinctive: embroidered in orange with a Khanda, the Sikh symbol, and below it, in Punjabi script, was the word Khalsa, meaning 'pure' — a troublesome notion in any language, and one which was being challenged simply by our atheist presence amongst the community of believers. There was nothing pure about that patka, not even the love that had prompted my mum to buy it at the Golden Temple in Amritsar as a gift. Her love for my husband — now so deep, so unreserved — had begun as dislike. Of all the early familial refusal of my attachment to him, my mother's was the most forceful, the most hurtful. Without even meeting him she'd spurned him, forbidden me from using his name in her presence — mainly because he wasn't the colour she had wanted for me. It took almost a year before they finally met and then, quickly, her feelings changed. What we love is the undesired.

My husband caught my eye and raised his brows. Should we go? I motioned, not sure that any langar was worth these interminable prayers in a Punjabi I barely understood. He shook his head. Soon the ardās started and I knew the end was near. Meanwhile, more and more people arrived and went up to bow before the Guru Granth Sahib before finding a spot on the floor in the crowded room. Clearly they knew how things worked here and had no compunction about arriving just in time to eat. Why was I so bothered about making a show of joining in the service first? I didn't know a soul here and would likely never come again. There was a wish to be polite — but this seemed superfluous in the context of the langar, which explicitly allows for anybody to eat, whether or not they attend the service. I felt some obscure guilt, a fear of being judged for taking something without giving. The small donation I proffered when bowing before the holy book was insufficient. I felt obliged to give my time because that was more precious to me — even though my sitting there was benefitting no one in any way and was only giving me hip ache.

All this made me wonder, how might it feel to be some place where there really are absolutely no conditions? If no code is imposed, don't you simply revert to the one you know?

Finally, a Granthi came around with parshad and dropped a warm, gelatinous ball of it in my palm. It was made with wholegrain wheat! I swallowed the smooth, saccharine pap and longed for the firmer consistency, the coarser texture, the supremely superior taste of the semolina version.

I noticed others standing and heading out immediately after getting their blessing, and I remembered what the man had told me on the phone: we don't have enough space, so people have to eat in shifts, but we manage to feed everyone somehow between two and four. I quickly rose as well and signalled to my husband to join me.

Downstairs, in a room adjoining the kitchen, people – still with feet bare and heads covered – were already seated cross-legged in rows on long mats laid out barely a metre apart along the white-tiled floor. As in the prayer hall, men and women were divided – something I had never seen in a gurdwara. It seemed to shrink the parameters of the beautiful idea of sitting and eating together without distinction. The separation was such an anomaly for me that I couldn't quite believe it and that may be why, when I saw there was no more free space on the men's side, I told my husband to come and sit with me on the women's side. He did, and ended up being the only man there. I wondered if somebody would remark on this, but no one made a fuss and not a bad glance came our way.

Soon the sewadars were going up and down the aisles between the eaters. Some handed out the typical stainless steel plates, spoons and tumblers; others followed with buckets of dhal and yoghurt, mixed vegetable sabzi and kheer, rice and rotis. *Dhal-ji, Waheguru-ji? Chawal-ji, Waheguru-ji?* they asked before scooping spoonfuls into waiting plates.

It was harder than I had anticipated to eat while sitting down, with your plate on the floor in front of you. I had to lean forward, tilting myself like a crane, to avoid dropping anything on my clothes. I glanced up: those around me were similarly angled over their food. The rows of bowed heads, draped in colourful cloth, bobbed like lines of bunting in the breeze.

There was an unspoken pressure to hurry so that those waiting – a queue snaked from the nearby door all the way upstairs to the prayer hall – could also have a bite. I picked at my black dhal and the yoghurt. Somewhere in the room I could feel my mother's reproving stare, the old warning not to waste it. Thank goodness my husband was seated right beside me. We swapped plates when he was done so that he could finish what I hadn't. All the while, I was distracted by the bare feet of neighbouring diners and of the servers as they passed: the smooth heels of the young, the uncut nails of some teenagers, the cracked soles and calloused knuckles of the old. The bunions, the lesions, the glisten of freshly painted polish on some toes and the sad, chipped colour on others. To consort with strangers is to accept uneasy intimacies.

There is a menial side to all hosting if you cook, serve and clean up yourself. Think of scraping away leftovers, of handling – if only en route to the dishwasher – used cutlery and glasses: your fingers touch where mouths pressed, tongues licked. We do this without rancour or repulsion for those we have invited, those we have chosen.

Sharing in the langar that day were a number of young Asian men who didn't wear turbans and who spoke Tamil, Bengali or Farsi. Some of them had appeared briefly in the prayer hall at the end of the service, but others had clearly headed straight for the dining room. None of this justifies an assumption that they were not there as followers of Sikhism – nevertheless, I suspected that, like me, they weren't. Nor, I felt sure, was the lone young white man who partook of the meal wearing a beret. How did these people find out about langar? How often did they come? I never got a chance to ask. The conditions at that gurdwara – the floor seating, the eating shifts – weren't conducive to conversation, and this diminished the hospitality somewhat.

'THE ONLY POSSIBILITY OF the thing is the experience of the impossibility.'

The European Union embodies, on a grand scale, Derrida's idea of the impossible as the condition for the possibility of something. A project to unite dozens of very different nations by opening borders, aligning economies and striving for equal rights and opportunities for hundreds of millions of citizens is utterly fantastic — in the sense that it is both implausible and magnificent.

I commuted for a decade between London and Berlin without asking anyone's permission or fulfilling any condition. In Germany, no one insisted I learn the language or questioned my values or insinuated I might be a burden on the state. Certainly, mine was a voluntary, privileged moving, cushioned by many factors, not least my language — English, the world's lingua franca. Still, millions in the EU have had a similar experience of welcome: travelling through twenty-eight EU member states without visas and, in the Schengen area, without showing passports, living almost anywhere in the union. Many of us have, without integration courses or citizenship tests, become exemplary Europeans, developing an identity simply through being allowed to live it.

At a time when the question of who has a right to be where, and under what conditions, is so vexed, the EU stands — in its ideals, if not always in its deeds — for a capacious conception of belonging. The spangled ring on its flag might, if you squint, appear as a halo of hospitality. Selective hospitality. For the model is defective, afflicted by inhospitable inclinations − as evidenced in the handling of Greek debt and of refugees. Nevertheless, the EU is still exceptional in the degree to which it has stretched our imagination.

All this is easy to forget at a moment when nationalism is being brazenly revived, its ugly, false rhetoric gaining easy traction in an environment where public discourse thrives on sensationalism. The promise of nationalism is impossible too, and the toll of its failures much higher, for nationalism is the opposite of unconditional hospitality, it always ends as unconditional hostility: the 'other' as *persona non grata*, regardless of biography, circumstances, international law or common decency.

As someone who'd rarely heard a good word about the EU in England, I was initially smitten by my experience of it through Germany. Some friends cautioned my rather starry-eyed view of the EU: just remember, they said, there is another Germany, another Europe. I had an inkling of what they meant. I'd glimpsed it in the question put to me most often, and most innocuously: *Where are you from?* Words that in their benign inquisitiveness revealed an utter narrowness about who was or could be German.

Still, it would be a while before I saw more sinister incarnations of such insularity. I was high on a new appreciation of democracy and freedom developed through various forms of political engagement in dEUtschland:

campaigning against mass surveillance, organising appeals for the release of Liu Xiaobo in China and Ashraf Fayad in Saudi Arabia. Such experiences extended my imagination of what it means to be and to belong in the world, how far allegiances might stretch. I began to conceive of belonging as a political condition rooted in commitment to a shared project and to values defined with and struggled for in concert with others. New rings of alliance and reliance formed, looping beyond the perimeters I had regarded as final, as the utmost that might be managed.

'The political realm', Hannah Arendt wrote, 'rises directly out of acting together, the sharing of words and deeds.' She used the Greek word *polis* to describe the group of citizens who assemble in this way. And she emphasises that 'the polis . . . is not the city-state in its physical location; it is the organisation of the people as it arises out of speaking and acting together, and its true space lies between people living together for this purpose, no matter where they happen to be.' In this way, many become one – a political 'body' created by collective concern, fed by common effort: a kind of cooperative hospitality, which is perhaps another way of saying a real democracy.

MY BELIEF IN THE necessity of the EU led me to launch a campaign for the establishment of a European public holiday across Europe. I always imagine it as a British-style bank holiday Monday, which would open up space for a long weekend marked by street parties and cultural events all over the continent. The idea occurred to me in the aftermath of Brexit when I was considering what possibilities British citizens had to explore and develop their own relationship with the EU. They had little room, I realised, between an education defined by a very selective, distorted view of history and a public discourse characterised by constant EU-bashing. The causes of Brexit are complex and an extra holiday wouldn't necessarily have altered the choice of those who voted out of dissatisfaction at worsening social and economic conditions. Nevertheless, the very existence of a European holiday would, I think, have marked the common consciousness in unexpected ways.

Holidays release us from the daily routine: they are an invitation to be and act different. Street parties have the power to seduce and connect; they bring out people who might not otherwise join in public occasions; they give us permission to come together in another spirit: to be wilder, freer. We need more means to counter the growing nationalist and illiberal tendencies in our societies. Why not use the power of celebration? Celebration as cultural and political intervention. Festivity as a form of dreaming, of discovery, of friendship. Festivity as an act of gratitude, of attention, of hospitality.

Nations fully utilise – if not always to noble ends – the

power of holidays, a power to create and entrench narratives, to foster love and loyalty for the things the state holds dear. The potential of a transnational, secular holiday is tremendous and it shocks me that the EU has not tried it.

One of the articles I wrote to outline the idea was published online, along with a photo of me standing beside the EU flag. In the piece I describe my discomfiture at posing with this 'symbol', which, like most existing EU emblems, feels empty and remote. I go on to describe how a European holiday could be a much more powerful, personal symbol for citizens. Soon there were a host of comments in response, a number of them insistent that I was *'gar keine Europäerin'* – no European.

'Priya Basil is a British-Indian writer. India is not in the EU and GB won't be either soon. So why is she going on about things that have nothing to do with her?'

There is another Germany.

'Best would be a shifting holiday that's tied to the end of Ramadan.'

'Why?' someone else asked. And I too wondered what had prompted the suggestion. I scrolled through my article re-reading, failing to make any connection. All the while, the commentary went on.

'Because if things go on as they are, the majority of people living in the EU in future will anyhow be Muslim?!'

I moved my mouse up and down the screen, ran my eyes over my words – which were not quite my words, because they were translated. And maybe this slight distance made me doubt, made me think I might have been unclear and thus caused a misunderstanding. Why else were so many of the comments fixated on Islam?

'In my opinion, stopping the current migration movement, e.g. protecting the EU's external borders, would do much more for community feeling than ten holidays.'

I could find nothing in my text, could trace no line between my proposal of a European holiday and the statements of these readers. Then, as the cursor swept once more over the page, I saw the picture of myself beside the EU flag – which was drooping, the circle broken, the stars out of line. Finally, I made the link: my brown face had triggered thoughts of migrants and Muslims.

There is another Germany.

Towards the end of the commentary chain, the person who proposed the end of Ramadan as a possible European holiday weighed in once more:

'There are Catholic and Evangelical public holidays, but no Muslim one. It would be a great signal that we accept the Muslims in our society.'

There are many Germanys.

DHAL-JI, WAHEGURU-JI? CHAWAL-JI, WAHEGURU-JI? The sewadars at the temple in Berlin chanted continuously as they did their circuits around the eaters, offering seconds, thirds and more.

In Punjabi the affix *–ji* indicates respect. It can be added to names or to nouns: Aunty-ji, Mum-ji, President-ji, Robert-ji. I had never heard it added to food. Yet it made sense to show esteem for the fare that was briefly nourishing and uniting strangers. The food, it seemed, was not just fostering community, it was in its own right a member of the community.

Honouring the sources of sustenance has been integral to the daily life of various peoples through time. It remains so in religions like Buddhism and in animist belief systems, especially amongst indigenous peoples. The Native American Lakota people have a profound, moving phrase: *Mitákuye Oyás'iß*. Part of a gratitude prayer, it translates as 'all my relations' and is used to acknowledge the interconnectedness of all life forms. For the Lakota people, 'relations' are not limited to your bloodline or wider human affiliations, but extend to everything you interact with, enjoy or use: strangers, animals, birds, insects, trees, plants, and even sun and stars, rocks and rivers, mountains and valleys.

If more of us maintained such a mind-set, perhaps we would not have plundered our planet quite so recklessly over the last decades. Since the mid twentieth century, farming has become ever more intensive: crop yields raised with the use of fertilisers, pesticides and other technologies; animals bred faster and fatter with the help of hormones and antibiotics. This was in some respects necessary to adequately feed the rapidly growing world population, which increased sevenfold between 1800 and 2000. Only half of the humans on earth at the end of the twentieth century could have been fed were it not for the Haber–Bosch process and the mass production of nitrates for fertiliser that it enabled – the very fertilisers whose creation produces noxious greenhouse gases, whose run-off from farming pollutes lakes and rivers. At least 70 per cent of the available fresh water on our planet is already exploited by us, with agriculture accounting for two-thirds of water use. The amount of fresh water available per person at the end of the twentieth century was only half of that in the middle of the century. About two-thirds of the population has experienced water shortages.

Only a quarter of the world population as a whole is now employed in agriculture. Much of that labour happens in countries that are less developed and more indebted. Figures released by the World Bank reveal that, on average, half the population in African countries work in agriculture – though the proportion varies dramatically across the continent: 6 per cent in South Africa, 38 per cent in Kenya, 69 per cent in Uganda, 91 per cent in Burundi. In India it's 43 per cent, in the US 2 per cent, in the UK and Germany only 1 per cent. And almost everywhere, the numbers are still going down. Small wonder then that so many of us have become utterly estranged from where and how what we eat is produced.

Food demand looks set to increase by 50 per cent by 2030, and then possibly double by 2050. Not only is there a growing number of people to be fed, people's appetites are growing too. In developed countries obesity is becoming widespread, while increasing affluence in developing nations means greater numbers of people are eating more of the foods that are more costly to produce. Meat consumption in particular has risen dramatically in countries like China and India where it is now a status symbol for the newly wealthy.

Scientists generally agree that decreasing meat consumption, especially red meat, would raise our chances of feeding everybody adequately in 2050 – and with a reduced impact on the environment. Yet meat maintains a strong hold on the common imagination of what it means to be well fed.

It's disconcerting to consider how far food is allied to destruction. Much of the produce available today involves hostility towards the environment in which it's grown and through which it's transported – and not just the physical environment. Food is a vital part of the economy and as such an arena where mismatched forces meet and compete: local food production and developing country markets are caught in a rigged game with international trade tariffs and the agricultural subsidies of wealthier nations. The food economy, set up to preserve old hegemonies, has created a system where some have few or no options and others too many. Figures collected by the World Health Organization and the United Nations from 2016 show that almost a billion people on our planet go hungry, while double that number are eating too much and becoming overweight or obese.

WHEN I FIRST BECAME vegetarian my principal worry was not how I would eat, but what I would serve guests. Offering purely veggie fare seemed too frugal, almost mean – even though this was what I enjoyed on a daily basis and relished when dished out to me by others. I tried to compensate for the new 'limitation' at our table by cooking elaborate, multi-course meals, as if this way people might not notice that it was just pumpkin soup with cheese and thyme scones, good old mushrooms tucked between layers of lasagne, simple strips of aubergine rolled around feta and pine nuts. With a natural tendency to over-cater – I am Mumji's granddaughter, after all – I went completely overboard for fear that guests might otherwise leave unsatisfied because they hadn't got what they were 'used to' – whatever that might be. As I saw that friends appreciated the food and happily returned for more, I lost my self-consciousness about our vegetarian table. Strange that meat continues to have such status when much of it is now mass-produced in the most cruel, ignoble, unhealthy ways and is then sold more cheaply than some vegetables. Sometimes, I still feel an occasional pang of inadequacy, like when I suddenly notice there's no cheese in any of the dishes I've made. The guests won't be satisfied! I start to panic, before reminding myself that cheese has many virtues, but dinner can be quite complete without it — especially if there's dessert.

I realise now that though I never learned all the etiquette rules my mum tried to teach, I involuntarily picked up a bigger lesson: that my quality as a woman depended largely on my ability to be a good hostess. This flawed notion defined the Indian women of my mother's class and generation in Kenya. Even women like my mother, who worked and excelled at different things, were trapped by the ideal of the domestic goddess — an ideal that persists despite all the waves of feminist struggle.

Though I still get great pleasure in cooking and feeding people well, I wish the act were less rooted in traditional gender roles, and I wish it didn't matter so much to me what impression I make on my guests. If I could care less, maybe I could cede more kitchen duties to my husband. Chopper and cleaner extraordinaire, perhaps he would become a great chef — if I let him. But in that sense, too, I'm like Mumji: I prefer to cook and complain. I can well imagine that for centuries many women have seethed with hostility as they tried to fulfil the expectations — theirs and others' — of hospitality.

THERE ARE STORIES — true ones, no doubt — of the unfortunate and the dispossessed finding sanctuary at a gurdwara. Still, as far as I've observed, it seems to be mainly Sikhs who volunteer to make langar and who show up to eat it. Over the years, international newspapers and magazines have published pieces about how tens of thousands of people — often up to 100,000 — dine daily for free at the Golden Temple in Amritsar. As a result, a number of tourists are always amongst the ranks of the diners. Otherwise, there too the majority are Sikhs — as are most of the residents in Amritsar. Maybe langar is less an example of unconditional hospitality than a confirmation of kin selection, the theory that all animals, including humans, are far more likely to be generous towards those with whom they share the most genetic, or other, attributes.

Who gives, who knows about, and who accepts the open invitation? Can an invitation really be deemed 'open' if it isn't actively advertised and widespread in the least likely quarters? How would gurdwaras react if there were suddenly more non-Sikhs than Sikhs coming for langar?

Perhaps they would introduce some restriction, as one

Tafel food bank did in Germany because over 70 per cent of the people turning up were 'foreigners'. The Tafeln are a non-profit, nationwide, volunteer-run network that seeks to reduce food waste by collecting leftovers donated by shops and restaurants and distributing them to people in need. There are currently 940 Tafeln in Germany and their work is financed entirely by private donations. In the city of Essen – which, of all things, means 'food' in German – the local Tafel, overwhelmed by growing demand, decided that, for a while, new membership cards would only be given to those with German passports. This action was defended on the grounds that fair and orderly distribution was only possible if there was 'an equal balance' of Germans and foreigners. It was claimed that young migrant men were pushing ahead of older Germans and putting the latter off coming to the Tafel at all. Of course, this is not a desirable situation, but excluding non-Germans hardly seems the best way to deal with it. The story was widely covered in the media and the food bank's decision was condemned as xenophobic; volunteers with good intentions were branded as Nazis. Even Angela Merkel weighed in to say she did not support the Essener Tafel's approach – an odd move, criticising an organisation that was making up for the state's shortcomings.

I WOULD LIKE TO invite you—

The first time I heard those words in a Berlin restaurant I didn't know what to make of them. While I was still puzzling over the seeming half-sentence from a friend, waiting for the next part, my husband, seated beside me, smiled and said thanks. Instantly, something appeared to be settled. Everyone went back to perusing the menu, and the friend exclaimed over the listed variations of white asparagus: 'Have you tried it?' Her eyes fixed on me. 'No? Then you have not yet truly arrived in Germany!'

How many times can you arrive in a country? I have lost count. Again and again you reach a new part of the place, again and again you are not completely there. For me, this is the case not just in Germany, where I have now spent most of my adult life. It is the same with Great Britain, where I am still a citizen, with Kenya, where I grew up, and with India, where I have never lived, but which is the land of my ancestors. I have not yet truly arrived, anywhere. And perhaps that's partly because countries too — for all their declarations of certainty, their favoured versions of history, their flaunting of national boundaries — have also not reached any fixed, final state.

'You must take the classic,' the friend pointed and read aloud, '*one pound (raw and unpeeled) 1A Beelitz asparagus with new potatoes, brown butter or Hollandaise sauce*. Go on, please. My treat.' It was when she said those words that I finally grasped the meaning of her initial remark, *I would like to*

invite you: she intended to pay for the meal we were about
to have.

I held the menu, unable to focus on the options, unsure
about the next move. It was like doing a dance and suddenly
realising part of the routine has been missed out: the
crucial sequence where you spin through the steps of guest
and host, round and round, before slowing down into the
mutually agreed pose.

The Indian part of me, habituated to boisterous battles
over the bill in restaurants, to grovelling before guests, felt
obliged to protest, resist, insist — *but, I would like to invite you!*
And if I was going to accept, I needed a chance to refuse
first, since in my family initially demurring is a way of
acknowledging the other's generosity. At the same time, the
British part of me — which never wants to think about money
and always hopes someone else will eventually mumble *Shall
we split the bill?* — was relieved, even a little impressed by this
decisive clarification well before the first bite. It seemed
very mature, very stereotypically German somehow — estab-
lishing order in advance of placing orders. As I reined in
my conflicting impulses, I started to fret about the impli-
cations of the offer: would it be okay to have a starter *and*
dessert? Should I pick a cheaper main course? Was it now
clear that next time we would pay? Or were some older
scales of exchange at play, a long chain of unspoken understanding: the intimacy of credit and debit that accrues in
any relationship, with a person or a place?

The friend, back then, was more my husband's than mine. The country, the language, the customs — all were more his. I was just a guest — and several times over: behind the invitation to dinner that evening was the invitation of love, which had brought me from London to Berlin to live with the man who would become my husband. Behind love was another exclusive invitation called 'freedom of movement', extended by the European Union, which enabled me to migrate within its borders without any restriction. Invitation folded into invitation, obligation into obligation — for to receive also means, somehow, to reciprocate.

My plate arrived, the pale spears on it looked like ghosts of asparagus, a far cry from the vivid green vegetable I knew. I too felt like a wan version of myself, beset by uncertainties that persisted like a lingering stiffness in my joints. Being comfortable as a guest depends on many things, not least a sense that the roles could be switched; even if never matched materially, you just need to know that you too could host the other in some mutually agreeable way. At that restaurant table in Berlin, it seemed I would never be able to adopt enough of anything, nor give enough of myself, to be more than a guest in the city. Not even white asparagus would change that.

IN THE SUMMER OF 2015, Merkel had signalled a national *I would like to invite you* to the refugees arriving on Europe's south-eastern shores. It was a powerful sign issued in the face of reluctance to take in refugees across much of the rest of the EU, issued despite ambivalence in Germany itself and outright resistance in her own party. Indeed, some accused Merkel of acting unconstitutionally – not asking parliament, but simply unilaterally deciding to keep Germany's borders open. Others hailed her choice as a humanitarian act and a momentous stand to uphold the fundamental principle of open borders within the EU. Perhaps because of the fraught context in which it came about, and the highly charged debate about immigration that followed and persists, Merkel's really was a half sentence that still remains incomplete: I would like to invite you – but I can't say for how long, or with whom, or on what terms.

Be my guest. This common English expression means 'do as you wish, feel free'. Yet this is rarely how we treat a visitor. Every invitation contains an unspoken code of admission. Sometimes, as is happening with Germany's judicial process for asylum, the code is made deliberately obscure, so complex as to confound the very notion of welcome. In order to keep the coalition government intact, and appease its more reactionary elements, in 2018 the German parliament agreed to the creation of the so-called Ankerzentrum. The word, which also means 'anchor centre', is an acronym for *Ankommen Entscheidung Rückkehr* – 'Arrival Decision Return'. The centres are intended as mass transit hubs to accommodate all asylum seekers, effectively immobilising them from the moment they reach Germany until their applications are approved, or they are deported – a process that can take up to two years. Anker reverses the previous policy of placing new arrivals in communities across the country, an approach that helped people connect, adjust and settle even as their claims were handled. The plan – apparently hatched to win back voters who have drifted to the far right – is driven by the belief that if the whole asylum process is streamlined this way deportations can be speeded up. All the new system actually does is anchor the state's target of 'return' to the fact of 'arrival': anyone who comes must, ideally, go back as quickly as possible. Thankfully, most of the sixteen federal states have resisted the establishment of such centres within their jurisdiction. Only Saxony and Bavaria accepted the plan, and so far only Bavaria has centres in operation – one in each of its seven administrative districts.

The hospitality of international law, defined by the Refugee Convention agreed in Geneva in 1951, is being undermined the world over through constant amendments to national laws, which proliferate with ever more clauses and sub-clauses that subvert the status of the stranger and narrow the scope of his/her rights.

The Essener Tafel eventually reversed its policy and once

again began offering food without distinction — while stressing that, ultimately, it is the state's duty to make sure no one goes hungry. 'We support people in need, so that with the money they save on groceries they can maybe take their kids to the pool or the movie theater for once,' the chairman of the local food bank said. 'If anyone here starved just because the Tafel didn't exist any more, something would be going very wrong in this country.'

HOSPITALITY, WERE I TO draw it, would be a series of potentially endless concentric circles extending outwards from each of us. In their crisscrossing and overlapping, in the expanse of their reach, might be the critical pattern of our time. A pattern revealing — just as contour lines on a map indicate the gradient of the land — the true topography of a society: its landscape of reciprocity, its borders of generosity, its peaks and depths of give and take.

Yet, however far those circles spread, unconditional hospitality remains outside their furthest perimeter. It lies, for the most part, in unknown territory, off the map.

THE SIKH UTOPIA OF universal welcome described to me by Papaji in my youth contradicted not just the world I lived in, but even what I'd seen at our local gurdwara. Its huge iron gate, painted cyan blue, was manned, as all gates were and still are across Nairobi, by an askari. Back then, the private guards were armed with a truncheon; these days, many carry guns. Whenever I saw it, the vast blue gate was locked shut. Within it there was a standard-sized door and it was through this we passed to enter and leave the temple precinct. Even this portal did not stand ajar, but was opened and closed by the askari as visitors came and went. The street just outside thronged with black Kenyans — the men who directed drivers into obvious parking spots for one bob, the kids who trailed you begging for one bob and the majority who were simply passing by en route to their own business. Did they know, I wondered, of the free meal on the other side of the gate? Did the askari know? Would he even let in anyone black without asking questions? Those who stepped into the gurdwara precinct were mainly people of Indian descent. Occasionally, they brought along someone of a different denomination, but rarely anyone with a different skin colour. So the gatherings were, for the most part, overwhelmingly, glaringly, homogenous.

If anybody could join in, how come everybody didn't? This was the conundrum I turned over and over in my young mind during visits to the temple in the aftermath of Papaji's revelation. Eventually, I put the dilemma to my mum: there were so many poor people outside and the gurdwara food was free for all, so why didn't the poor come in to eat? After a pause, she said: 'They probably don't know about it. And anyhow, there wouldn't be enough for all of them.' This seemed reasonable: of course there were too many others, of course you couldn't help them all. At the same time, the logic felt flawed. Only looking back now can I articulate the question I should have asked next, but did not have the capacity to: surely there is some other option in between everybody coming or almost nobody?

IF HOSPITALITY IS A set of concentric circles, then each circumference is a set of conditions.

Life is conditional.

Meanwhile, its compass spins, the needle spiralling in every direction, but pointing, always, towards unconditional. There. There. There – almost-graspable-always-beyond-reach – the radical appeal to live as though every single life matters equally.

Impossible. Possible.

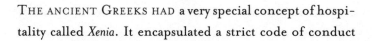

THE ANCIENT GREEKS HAD a very special concept of hospitality called *Xenia*. It encapsulated a strict code of conduct between guest and host, and involved each showing the utmost respect and consideration towards the other, especially if they were complete strangers.

As in many ancient cultures, the Greeks believed that gods mingled amongst humans. Since any seeming stranger could be a god in disguise, it was all the more necessary to offer that person unconditional hospitality and avoid the potential wrath of the gods. The idea may seem quaint to a modern sensibility, dosed, as we regularly are in the public realm, by fear about unknown others. In the West it manifests as conflation of immigrants with terrorists, dark skin with foreignness. Such othering has its ugly variants the world over.

Don't talk to strangers. This, I'll vouch, is how most children now first encounter the word 'stranger'. Far from treated as a being worthy of reverence, the unknown individual is, from the first, to be regarded with suspicion, kept at a distance. *Don't talk to strangers.* There may be some merit in the caution, but that surely dissolves when it becomes a permanent precaution for life. I lived like that in Kenya, and it was a diminished existence.

A recent national advertising campaign in India urging locals to respect tourists used a mantra from the Upanishads as its strapline: *Atithi Devo Bhava,* The Guest is God. In our times, it seems, only the stranger with money is god, worthy of a decent, dignified welcome. The rich can go everywhere, buy everything – even citizenship. The poor must get on vessels that are barely seaworthy, and be prepared to die in order to have anything.

The very meaning of the word *hospitality* in English has altered dramatically. It is now most commonly used as a prefix to *industry* and constitutes a vast commercial realm, from hotels and restaurants to spas and theme parks. Hospitality industry. An oxymoron? What does it say about us when a notion that long implied giving without getting any return becomes synonymous with paying for services that promise customer satisfaction or your money back?

Lady Chic, that finishing school my mum ran in Kenya back in the 1980s, seems – from my contemporary, feminist vantage point – old-fashioned in many respects. The social niceties the women learned – how to correctly lay a table, cook elaborate meals, look your best – gleaned from old etiquette books, served to uphold the very power structures that oppressed them, and which many came to the school to temporarily escape. Yet, the scheme was ahead of its time in how it unwittingly anticipated, in a tiny way, the evolution of hospitality. The art of hosting, which was ultimately what the women were aiming to excel at, was called 'entertaining'. Pretty much what the hospitality industry is all about today.

There's nothing wrong with entertainment per se. What troubles me is the damage it's wreaked on the notion of hospitality. In the clutches of 'industry', which is to say capitalism, hospitality has been commodified and become largely the prerogative of those who pay. And this idea of the privilege of the payer has gradually become a mentality that manifests in the most unlikely and unseemly places. In the UK it's evident in the recent demonising of the unemployed. People who for whatever reason – mental illness, disability, bad luck, recession-linked cuts – can't contribute financially to society are portrayed as parasites, not worthy of our compassion or the state's care, and therefore not deserving of the benefits to which they were previously entitled. Immigrants, despite overwhelming evidence that they contribute more to the British economy than they withdraw, have been disparaged for 'taking advantage' of the National Health Service. During the EU referendum, people were encouraged to 'take control' on the back of a promise that paying less to the EU, and barring foreign non-payers from the country, would mean more for British payers. Under the Tories, politics – infested by the jargon of industry – is all about 'delivering better value [for taxpayers]', not about living better values.

The fabric of decency is unravelling particularly fast and frighteningly in Europe, but intolerance is on the rise the world over, fuelled by growing social and economic inequality. Politics, which ought to help mitigate these developments, is right now itself beset by polarisation; indeed, in many places, it is politics which are responsible for its proliferation, even in supposedly 'mature' democracies such as the UK and the USA. In both countries, the lumbering two-party system increasingly leads to issues either stagnating or escalating. While each side blames the other, hostility holds hostage any impulse towards the consensus necessary for a more hospitable politics.

Yet these factors alone do not adequately account for the fervent right-wing claims of victimhood, their clamour to prioritise 'us' over 'them'. An 'us' based, for the most part, on wilfully ignorant assumptions. A lack of historical knowledge also contributes to claims of supposedly pure lines of descent from supposedly original settlers in a given territory. Such claims are used to justify sweeping judgements, hate speech and attacks on strangers who are never regarded as individuals, but as part of a threatening mob. Meanwhile, we ourselves want our individuality to be acknowledged, celebrated, protected. In the public sphere right now, sadly, corporations do this best, using data collected on us to engineer ever more carefully targeted marketing on- and offline, and thus offer us ever more − superficially − personal treatment.

Our food culture reflects these developments. Menus, those abstract maps of morality − who eats what, where and for how much − can, increasingly, also be read as small scrolls of specialness, or atlases of affliction, depending on how you prefer to see it. Many a *carte* now comes complete with a curious culinary cryptography: WF, GF, DF, N, V, VG, C are just some of the acronyms you might find on an average menu. A display of tolerance for common food intolerances. Such willingness to accommodate people's sensitivities and preferences jars with the growing unwillingness in many societies to, literally, accommodate others — that is to say, 'foreigners'. It seems we're becoming more hospitable and inhospitable at the same time. The hospitality industry, again, bears some responsibility for this since it thrives on the message that *you* are the only one who counts: you should come first, your every need considered and catered for. You deserve it, after all, as long as you can pay.

The continual championing of the individual inevitably diminishes the scope of the communal and may well further alter our notions of what it means to be hospitable. The use of robots for elderly care, already commonplace in Japan, is being tried in other developed nations. Artificial Intelligence is also being avidly advanced, not least for its enticing promise of ever more individually tailored experiences and services. What sort of people might we become, living with machines that grant us whatever we want without seemingly requiring anything in return — except our data?

Technology is giving a new charge to the word 'unconditional'. An exceptional, effort-full state of unlimited giving is being rendered ordinary and automatic through inventions like sexbots. These humanoid machines, targeted at heterosexual men (so far the industry has focused almost exclusively on producing robot women for men), offer a partner who, in the words of one creator, 'won't complain and is ready [for sex] 24/7'. Another inventor, from the company True Companion, says the sexbot is there 'to provide unconditional love and support. How could there be anything negative about that?'

Sex, one of the most intimate arenas of human reciprocity, is a sphere in which conditions should always apply — the terms not necessarily pre-determined, but mutually agreed every single time by those involved.

A BRITISH CHOCOLATE ADVERT from the 1980s has had a lasting influence on me. I didn't like the brand in question, but I was enchanted by the idea used to promote it. In the simple animated sketch, a couple are sitting on a bench. She's eating Rolos and he looks on longingly. 'It's my last one!' she protests, but then immediately offers it to him, saying, 'But you can have it anyway.' The famous brand strapline then follows: *Do you love anyone enough to give them your last Rolo?*

I often pictured myself as one half of such an amorous pair, though in my imaginings I was, without exception, the one receiving the last chocolate.

For much of my life I've contrived to get a bit, if not the most, or the rest, of whatever I like best. I'm the kind of person who organises leftovers before the meal's even started. There have been tantrums and tears when one of my siblings has unwittingly (or deliberately?) eaten my painstakingly preserved portions.

Through some extraordinary and, I sometimes feel, unearned stroke of luck – or fate, call it what you will – I met a man who will let me have not just the last bite, but the first, and every one in between. In a restaurant he'll happily swap dishes with me even if his choice is obviously superior. When we're sharing he'll gladly let me have more. 'Don't you mind?' I sometimes ask, and at the assurance that he doesn't I still wonder: 'But how can you not?'

'It doesn't matter to me the way it does to you,' he says.

'How is that possible?'

'Food is not the most important thing.'

'It's not just about food. It's taste, pleasure, satisfaction.'

'I get that too, in a different way, from seeing you enjoying it.'

I recall Nabokov's line in *Lolita*: 'It was love at first sight, at last sight, at ever and ever sight.' Then, I think of my husband and a delicious variation on the sentence comes to mind: love at first bite, at last bite, at ever and ever bite.

THE SIGNIFICANCE OF THE last piece differs depending on the size of the circle. An act that's agreeable, permissible or forgivable within the tight coil of two may not pass muster in a larger round, though strange pacts can be made within the bounds of a family. A friend told me how, when he was growing up in Harz, the family finances permitted meat only once a week – and then only for one person. It was the father who always got the meat, but my friend and his two brothers had the 'privilege', on alternating weeks, of feasting on the bones of their dad's leftovers. So every three weeks, my friend would get a few scraps of chicken or lamb. The two sisters never got a look in. Then, when he was twelve, my friend went to summer camp. On the first night, at dinner in the canteen, half a chicken was put on his plate. He stared in disbelief at the fleshy thigh, the crisp browned skin – then asked the woman serving: 'Is that for me?' And when she concurred, he still had to clarify: 'All of it?'

A family can, for the most part and at least for a while, function despite such imbalances. But the bigger a community gets, the clearer the rules of reciprocity need to be for a sense of fairness to be sustained. The intimacy of coupledom, though, allows for a singular understanding about – or, at the very least, a unique if awkward accommodation on – sharing. Yet we're so quick to judge pairs on how their life and love appears to be divided: whatever the balance, it mostly looks unequal to the outside eye.

Between my grandparents, Mumji and Papaji, it was the other way around: the divisions were numerous and impossible to grasp from the surface. Mumji spent the first half

of her married life cooking to impress Papaji and the
second half cooking to oppress him. She seemed to believe
that by deciding what went on his plate she could rule all
his appetites. When her food failed to turn him into the
totally compliant, doting man she wanted, she decided it
would keep him from being the completely open, inde-
pendent man he wished to be. Well into her seventies, his
eighties, she went on preparing three meals a day. She still
cooks as though expecting guests for every meal, and then
ends up freezing all the food. She has four freezers: two
in her kitchen, and two outside in the garage, including
one chest freezer large enough to store the bodies of two
men stacked atop each other. Every freezer is full, the cargo
furred with ice crystals. Who will eat it? Maybe when she
dies, the whole family will gather and defrost all the
contents and feast for a week. And everything, salted by
tears and leavened by memory, will taste fabulous, and she
will come alive once again in our mouths and nostrils, and
we'll hear her voice in our heads urging us to eat more,
to dupp to our hearts' (dis)content.

Putting food on the table now is, and was also in Papaji's
time, Mumji's way of filling the hours, of expressing a
need that had no other outlet. It was also a way of ensuring
Papaji returned home at mealtimes from his various voluntary jobs or visits to one of his four brothers who lived
nearby. The regime was her choice, but it didn't stop her
complaining that she was a slave to his hunger. He hated

her attempts at control, and yet turned up and tucked into every meal with relish, frequently declaring her 'the best cook ever'. She needed this validation like a daily vitamin. Neither was happy with their arrangement, and yet they made accommodations within it and managed to take care of each other, not emotionally or intellectually, but physically, practically. I hesitate to suggest that's enough, because it wouldn't be for me, and I don't believe it was for either of them. Such halfway hospitality damages, even if you permit it, even if you survive it.

Where had it gone wrong? At too many points to count. The most critical may be that she never told him about the illegitimate child. He found out from someone else, but never spoke to her about it. Their bond was wasted by silence, by the obvious unstated. I was naïve enough, when I started writing, to think I could fix what had festered for decades. I would tell the secret in a novel, and within the great embrace of literature all would be resolved. Yes, stories offer hospitality, but not the kind everyone wants to accept, least of all when told in a version they deem incorrect.

NOW AND THEN A thought niggles at me: the ones who readily give up the last Rolo – do they love more selflessly? Or are they just less greedy?

Jacques Derrida: Hospitality should be neither assimilation, acculturation, nor simply the occupation of my space by the Other. That's why it has to be negotiated at every instant, and the decision for hospitality, the best rule for this negotiation, has to be invented at every second with all the risks involved, and it is very risky . . . It is the responsibility of the other, but of the other in me before me. Of the other as me.

Hélène Cixous: It is an absolute yes to the other, and totally blind. You take on something of which you cannot measure the development, the effects, the destiny. You cannot do otherwise.

DURING THE COURSE OF my life, I have migrated from Nairobi to London to Berlin. In every instance, I chose to leave and anticipated welcome. Somehow, amazingly, all the transitions were pretty smooth and it's probably because I never went as a complete stranger. There was always someone to mediate my way in the new place and, particularly in Germany, to shield me from the initial difficulties of not knowing the language or forms. In the summer of 2015, I found myself part of a society into which people were suddenly arriving in numbers I couldn't help but notice. Hundreds of thousands of refugees fleeing war and persecution sought haven in Europe and found only a handful of countries willing to receive them.

Almost every woman I met in Berlin at that time told stories of the ways, big and small, in which they were assisting the newcomers. Around three-quarters of those involved in the nationwide civic effort to welcome refugees were women. No surprise there. Throughout history, work that involves caring for or assisting others has mostly been done by women, often through imposition and necessity rather than choice. Indeed, much of the initial volunteer activity in Germany that summer was a consequence of the state's failure to respond adequately. Some said this incompetence was deliberate, a tactic to put off more arrivals. The authorities themselves asserted it was accidental, a case of being unprepared and overwhelmed by the sheer scale of arrivals. Whatever the verity of those claims, what's indisputable is the fact that many citizens turned their front rooms into overnight shelters for strangers or paid for hotel rooms where they could stay. They cooked hot meals, then went and served them to those waiting for hours in the cold outside the single registration centre. They took sick refugees to their own doctors. I felt like the odd one out; all I'd done was collect and donate clothes from the residents of our apartment block. So I eagerly joined in when a group of women I knew decided to try to harness all the positive energy in the wider society, and also work with the newcomers, to forge a better future. We founded an initiative called WIR MACHEN DAS, WE'RE DOING IT – a dynamic extension of Angela Merkel's pragmatic *Wir Schaffen Das*, We'll Manage It.

Surround yourself by people who are better than you that they may raise you up, so the common wisdom goes. I was lifted by many incredible women who practised a form of *Xenia*, engaging with the refugees as with gods; that's to say individuals deserving of whatever assistance or opportunity that could be granted them in circumstances where so much had been taken away, and so much was still denied. These were women who viewed migration as an opportunity to catalyse the urgent work of re-shaping our societies and to foster a broader culture of equality and sharing. These women countered the clamour for an immigration cap with calls for a migrant minimum: *You think one million is too many? Really? We want one million every year!* These women demanded higher standards from themselves and the entire society when the political and popular impulse was to lower the bar by reducing legal protections for refugees or disparaging migrants with lies and coarse language. WIR MACHEN DAS established cultural, legal and journalistic projects focused on giving newcomers the means to express themselves. The initiative opened up spaces where the newcomers could meet Germans on as equal a footing as possible.

The experience of working for WIR MACHEN DAS has been one of the most enriching of my life, and also one of the most challenging. I found myself caught in a strange bind: desiring something and fearing it, celebrating something and doubting it, doing something as a way of not doing its opposite.

THOUGH MY CHILDHOOD WORRIES about there not being 'enough' in the world have diminished, now and then, in the midst of a comfortable existence, I experience all kinds of scarcity angst.

Sometimes we imagine things that we know can never be admitted to anybody. Sometimes we have thoughts that we would rather not admit, but which we end up confessing for all manner of reasons, perhaps because we need to be chastened or forgiven or reassured — or simply to be heard. The fear had been in me for weeks before I mentioned it to my husband. Even as I brought it up, I skirted around it.

'You're going to think I'm awful,' I warned.

'You know I could never think that.'

I didn't quite believe him, even though I had entrusted my worst fears to him before and he had listened without belittling them or condemning me.

'This is really bad,' I said. 'You'll be shocked at how selfish and insecure I am.'

'What is it?' His face grew serious with concern.

I shook my head, tried to change the subject. This was really one of those instances, I told myself, when it was better not to say.

'Just tell me.'

I had his full attention. It beamed from him, benevolent, expansive, reliable. I felt the weight of my terrible thoughts, but more than that I apprehended the wondrous gift of love, ready to grant me a generous audience.

'I can't help thinking,' I began — then stopped again. In my mind I saw the refugees I had met. 'With so many more attractive, intelligent people here,' I continued, 'I won't be so unique. No one will be interested in me any more.'

'I don't understand. You are and always will be unique, regardless of whoever else is there.'

I tried to explain, more mortified by every word I uttered, just as I am now with every word I write. I had got used to being the exception. It disturbed me to realise that my skin colour had again become a distinguishing feature. In Kenya it had denoted a second-class status, a consequence of the confused colonial mentality that left people like my parents accepting that Indians were 'inferior' to whites and 'superior' to blacks. Now here I was in Germany experiencing (imagining?) an odd sort of distinction for being brown.

'As Germany becomes ever more multi-cultural,' I said, 'there will be so many other people here who have the

94

experience of living between different worlds, who can reflect German society back to itself through a different lens. I know that's a good thing. But I'm scared that I'll just become extraneous.'

An even pettier version of this fear had haunted me before, the concerns billowing briefly each time I read or heard about how many international artists, especially writers, were moving to Berlin: I won't be so unusual any more, I'll be less in demand. In fact, over the years, as the numbers of other artists in the city grew, so did my own opportunities. The one had nothing to do with the other. There is enough space in the world for everyone's success. Again and again I remember this. Again and again I forget it.

'Think of your particular biography,' my husband said, 'your Indian, Kenyan, British and now German background. Consider all the things you've read, all the things you've written and done. It's this mixture that makes you what you are. You're distinguished simply by being you – with your own particular constellation of knowledge and experience, your own sensitivities, limitations and oddities, your own particular way of expressing these. No one can take any of that away from you.'

I wanted to believe him, but the faith was weak, wavering. Then I read Hannah Arendt and believed a little more.

'We are all the same,' Arendt wrote in *The Human Condition*, 'that is, human, in such a way that nobody is ever the same as anyone else who ever lived, lives, or will live.' She called this 'plurality' and defined it as the basic condition for all human action.

PLATO'S LATE DIALOGUES ARE composed of exchanges with a 'stranger' or 'foreigner'. They show how it is through interaction with an 'other' that thought is best challenged and extended. In the Socratic tradition, from which Plato emerged, that 'other' can also be oneself. Thinking at its most productive and exciting is transgressive, it involves pushing boundaries, changing positions – it can put you at odds with yourself. Philosophy, in a way, is a long story of being at home amidst contradiction and complexity.

MISTAKES, MISHAPS, MISUNDERSTANDINGS, BIG or small, are the training ground of hospitality. A friend told me of his faux pas on first meeting the family of his future Danish wife. They went to her parents' home near Copenhagen for tea. A freshly baked cake, still pristine, was served. As the guest, my friend was the first to be handed the knife. He accepted and, following his German proclivity, proceeded to equally portion up the entire cake, chatting all the while, oblivious to the looks of dismay

being exchanged between the family members. Only afterwards did he learn that in Denmark you don't cut a slice
for others, certainly not without asking. People should be
allowed to cut for themselves, to take as much or as little
as they want.

When I first started cooking and having people over for
dinner, I enjoyed plating each individual portion, making
it look as elegant as in a fancy restaurant. Only after many
instances where people did not finish, did it occur to me
that my aesthetic pleasure was also a kind of autocratic
measure against which some had to rebel even at the risk
of appearing impolite.

The guest submits to the whims of the host. On
receiving an invitation you don't — or rarely — ask who
else will be there and what will be served. You abdicate
responsibility, try to arrive on time, accept where you're
seated, eat what you're given. If there's a buffet you don't
want to be the first to help yourself. You may hesitate to
ask for salt if the food is bland. You don't dwell on the
possibility of vegetables prepped by unwashed hands, or
slivers of onion that slipped to the floor before being
salvaged and thrown into the soup, or sucked fingers
dipped repeatedly in sauces to check seasoning. Your
choices are constrained and, therefore, it seems reasonable that you should at least be able to decide how much
goes on your plate. I now prefer to lay out dishes and let
people help themselves.

There's one thing people generally avoid taking – the last portion of any shared dish. So common is this custom across cultures that there are words for it in different languages. In Swedish it's known as *en trivselbit*, 'comfort piece'. In German *das Anstandstück*, 'decency piece'. In Spanish *la vergüenza*, 'the shame'. In the Arab world it's common to leave an uneaten morsel on your plate as a signal to the host that you've been served enough, more than you could finish. A similar custom prevails in China, though there the last piece has other meanings too. Some leave a bite of every meal uneaten in memory of the times when food was so scarce you wouldn't waste the tiniest speck. The Chinese also have an understanding that one should never help oneself to the last piece of a shared dish without asking the others first, nor refuse when offered it. My mother tried to ingrain a similar notion in me, one of the few universal and enduring rules of her etiquette training. In America *mannersbit* was once used to signify the convention of restraint when it comes to tasty last titbits. Nowadays in the Anglo-American sphere, you're more likely to hear someone claim the final bit of food with nary a qualm: 'Can't leave just one.' 'Do you mind if I kill that?' 'You don't want this, do you?' Which says a lot about evolving notions of propriety.

Be My Guest

I'M USUALLY CAUGHT SOMEWHERE between a wish to be gracious and a tendency to be rapacious when it comes to last bites. I doubt I could live up to the standards of an ancient Chinese wisdom that has its counterpart in cultures the world over: a well-raised person eats in such a way that the others at the table wouldn't notice what his favourite dish is. If I've sometimes followed this dignified practice it's been for the most undignified ends. When a box of chocolates is passed around in our family and I've picked one that I especially like, I'll give no sign of my luck or relish in the hope that nobody else will take the second sample of my preferred variety. As a kid, I used to make disgusted faces and pretend I'd picked a dud so that my sister would choose something entirely different and I could then triumphantly grab the same chocolate all over again.

'Why do you assume that what you like is the best?' my husband wonders, startling me with the obvious fact that we all have different tastes. Still, I have to hold back from meddling as others eat: not dictate that there should be pumpkin seeds in each bite of salad because I love the crunchy contrast; not insist on pouring more tahini sauce over the lentils because I love them doused. My husband doesn't escape such advice, of course. When it gets too much, he'll set down his fork and ask me, very politely: 'Would you like to eat my dinner for me?'

THERE'S ONE BITE I never ever want to have, let alone think about: the final bite of something my mother has cooked when she is no longer there to make more. I save some of the tarka she gives me in any one batch until I've got the next lot, so that whatever happens there will always be the chance of one more Mum-cooked meal. Part of me wants to have multiple freezers like Mumji, all filled to bursting with my mum's concoctions. Kadhi tarka ad infinitum.

IT COMES ON THICK white card, embossed with a glittering eagle — the standard of the Federal President, written in gold letters: *Sie sind eingeladen* . . . The most formal invitation I have ever received, the most official — asking me to take part in an occasion to mark the hundredth birth anniversary of Heinrich Böll, one of Germany's most revered writers and political figures, a hero to President Frank-Walter Steinmeier.

Does this mean, somehow, that I've arrived?

I call the lady responsible for organising the event, thank her for asking me and then admit I'm not sure my German is up to it. 'No problem, feel free to talk in English,' she says without missing a beat. 'The other two participants will speak German,' she continues, 'but you must do whatever makes you comfortable.' So I accept, and at once begin studying as though for an exam: of course I have to do it in German — because that, for all its discomforts, is, in my judgement, the most suitable thing. It is my way of being more than a guest.

On stage at the event in the Villa Hammerschmidt I speak, for the first time since coming to Germany, only German — an odd version, dressed in an English accent and adorned with grammar mistakes. Fluent but flawed, I tell a friend later and she says: 'Isn't that our condition, whatever language we speak?'

IN *THE LIFE YOU Can Save* Peter Singer shows how levels of giving rise all round when people see how much others are doing. He describes, for instance, how contributions to a cause went up during the course of a radio show that kept announcing who had just given and what amount. Perhaps it helped that the names included celebrities. Just as we're influenced by a friend's handbag or a neighbour's car, we can be inspired by their acts of altruism. It's just that flaunting philanthropy has not — on the whole (there are always those who want their name very publically emblazoned on any endowment) — been deemed sexy, let alone permissible. *The left hand should not know what the right has given.* Some version of this dictum, so explicitly stated in Christian and Islamic scriptures, seems to pervade most beliefs about charity. Many are reluctant to admit what they give for fear of seeming worthy or self-righteous. Peter Singer suggests we banish such bashfulness and openly discuss donation in order to encourage and motivate one another to do more of it. I think the same goes for activism and political engagement.

There was certainly some healthy sharing contagion in all the tales about citizens engaging with refugees in Germany. For a while, the media were full of it too: reports teemed with the term *Willkommenskultur*, coined to describe the enthusiastic reception of the new arrivals by many Germans. Then, suddenly, there was a shift: a handful of refugee crimes, committed by a tiny proportion of those who came, served to change the narrative. Volunteers were still out in force, but no one was interested in them any more. Notes of caution and doubt, and too often of hysteria, crept into reporting on migration, until it seemed as though a *Willkommenswarnung* was being issued. Huge numbers of repugnant right-wing voices began to join the anti-immigration chorus, and to commit crimes against refugees and those who helped them. This extreme faction even ended up being elected into parliament in 2017 – for the first time in more than half a century an extreme right-wing, some would say neo-Nazi, party was in the Bundestag.

Here was that other Germany again – except even those who'd long warned of its existence had not anticipated it would re-emerge into the mainstream with such confidence and venom, recruit followers with such speed and success. I could – to a point – understand the kinds of fear leading people to seek security in fantasy promises that change could be halted, society restored to some bygone idyll of sameness. But my sympathy stalled at the sound of these claims, their blatant falseness, their racist thrust.

The far right everywhere often seems more consolidated, or at least it is more readily mobilised as a crowd and thus able to project more unity and get greater media visibility. At WIR MACHEN DAS we are convinced that there is a counter-crowd, a grass-roots force that can help reverse the rising fascism – if only it could be seen, and perhaps even see itself, as a movement. We organised a conference at the House of World Cultures in Berlin and hosted representatives of almost one hundred different NGOs involved with migration or refugee issues all around Germany. I was one of those who quixotically imagined that we would find a way to unite our efforts, express ourselves as one and thus make a greater impact. But we kept disagreeing over modes and methods, emphasising contrasting priorities, even if, ultimately, our objective was a diverse, inclusive society. It became resoundingly clear that for all the goodwill, the shared goals of those who came together, the struggles for different rights – queer, Muslim, black, Afghan, gay, Roma and more – needed to remain separate.

Make yourself at home. One of the warmest entreaties anyone can be given. To be at home is to be able to be yourself. The insistence on staying distinct, as expressed by all the initiatives gathered at the conference, illustrated an instance of the perpetual effort required by any group to make itself at home in a diverse society – and make that society comfortable with it. For the far right, to be at home means to conform to some pre-existing, rigid idea. *Make yourself at home* is their order to fit in, to assimilate – as if people are pieces of furniture that can be arranged to match an old décor.

A democracy, in essence, should house difference, shelter diversity, welcome novelty. No nation state on its own can be democratic in the fullest sense of the word, because to be a nation is to be more or less nationalistic, which is to say, more or less exclusionary. That's why the EU remains vital as an ongoing effort to subordinate the national to a wider civic space, where more and more people of every kind can be at home. Yet that very EU is now trying everything to seal itself off from those not already inside. What astonishes me most are not the heinous measures – paying Turkey to keep refugees who want to travel from its shores, paying African dictators to prevent people leaving the continent – but the misplaced belief that others can be permanently kept out.

Derrida acknowledged, 'I cannot say that I open the doors, that I invite the other: the other is already there. That is unconditional hospitality (foreign to politics and law, even to the ethical in the narrow sense). Hospitality of visitation and not invitation. The other has already entered, even if he is not invited . . . This is what we have to deal with.'

IN THE SUMMER OF 2017, an older, white man shoved into me on the street in Berlin, then shouted: 'Why did you do that?' He threatened to call the police, before leaning in close and, with his face barely centimetres from mine, declared: 'I hate you.'

At one stroke, the country where I'd felt most accepted also became the place where I was most publically rejected. What shocked me about the encounter was the hatred the man exuded. What shocked me more, later, was that I didn't believe he was talking to me. I couldn't accept that my mere presence in the street could so disgust and enrage another person. And so — even though it was me the man pushed into, my face that he thrust his own towards — I told myself, at first, that everything he said was directed at the person with me, a fellow writer, a black man.

You try to unlearn prejudice beat by beat, correcting yourself each time it pulses to the fore. Sometimes it's there before you can stop it, tapping out its false lore, tripping you into its trap.

There were two racists in the street that day. The difference between them was simply that one didn't want the other to be at all. While one didn't want to be at all racist, but kept finding leftovers of prejudice in herself.

JUST AS AN ALCOHOLIC who quits drinking is still considered an alcoholic, only a sober one, so a racist who tries to desist from racism remains, nevertheless, a sober racist. How could it be otherwise when we're steeped in social, political and legal structures shaped by bigotry, when we're raised on intoxicating stories of supposed superiority, and routinely offered the cheap cocktail of historical denial?

SOME EUROPEAN COUNTRIES HAVE tried to deal with the uninvited stranger by criminalising hospitality: citizens who've helped migrants have been prosecuted for the offence of people smuggling, volunteer organisations banned from distributing food to refugees.

When I think of the EU now I see it ringed by a huge blue gate. A gate that never opens, but contains a small door through which the select few may pass. I knew a gate like that once. Sometimes, it feels like I'm back where I started, part of a community that professes great universal ideals, declares these the right of every human being, but can't then extend them in a fair or generous way.

Nations have etiquette books of a kind too: constitutions, international conventions, charters of rights. These may not be perfect, but they are anchors that can help prevent societies drifting too far from decency. Finally, it's citizens who bear the brunt when countries behave badly. In its drive to secure Europe's shores from non-Europeans, the EU is undermining its own unique and beautiful etiquette of openness. Barring others from coming to Europe is but a short step to barring Europe from coming to us — Brexit is the case in point.

Chicken Tikka Masala has long topped lists of Britain's favourite national dish, but now there's a small curry crisis in the country. Changes to immigration rules have made it more difficult to bring skilled workers from abroad, resulting in a shortage of chefs with the culinary skills to run an Indian-style kitchen. It's also harder to find staff for new restaurants and existing ones because most English people aren't keen on doing that kind of work. Moreover, many second and third generation immigrants no longer wish to follow their families into the food business.

Surely there is some other option in between everybody coming or nobody? That question of my past remains the question of my present, of our present.

How might we respond to the reality of more and more people on the move? Besides doing better on upholding the right to political asylum, it seems to me the EU must also actively reach out towards those in less stable or wealthy lands who wish to live, as we do, in freedom, security, prosperity and peace. This could be done through a European Green Card Lottery run along the lines of the American model. People from all over the world apply, and every year the EU gives resident visas to 100,000 people from countries deemed to have low rates of immigration to our continent. The newcomers would be settled across Europe according to a pre-agreed quota system. This arrangement would be fair to others, while giving member states the chance to do background checks and prepare a smooth settlement process. As the system becomes established, the number of visas granted should be continually raised.

AT THE BEGINNING OF *The Physiology of Taste*, the French epicure Brillat-Savarin meditates on the different senses, which he describes as 'the organs by which man places himself in connection with exterior objects'. He asserts that 'there are at least six'. To taste, sight, smell, sound and touch he adds physical love, claiming it is by dint of this pull that our species reproduces and therefore – I assume, though he doesn't explicitly say this – can continue to try to gratify all other senses. He argues that physical love cannot be conflated with touch since it has its own particular 'apparatus' of sensation 'as complete as the mouth or the eyes'. Having instated this sixth sense, however, he says little more about it. Exploring the erotic aspects of food might lead first to lists of aphrodisiacs and then quickly into the realm of fetish, which may be why Brillat-Savarin avoided it. Writing today, what might he have made of the contemporary #foodporn phenomenon?

One of the most popular hashtags on social media, #foodporn comprises countless food-focused photos and videos intended to stimulate food envy and arouse the appetite. The majority seem to showcase triple-stacked burgers, overloaded pizzas and multi-layered desserts. There still isn't much conclusive research on how this surfeit of sexy snack-shots is affecting the eating habits of the mostly millennials who post and share them. Maybe looking at so much calorific food dulls hunger. I've sometimes leafed through numerous cookbooks wondering what to bake, only to find I no longer feel like making a cake.

At the other end of the social media culinary spectrum is #eatclean. Here the array of images includes berry smoothies, shots of wheatgerm, salad bowls, avocado toast (on gluten-free bread) and many pictures of trim, toned bodies. The food writer Bee Wilson describes the phenomenon as 'an attempt to offer a new way of eating that comes without any fear or guilt', and concludes that the movement represents a dysfunctional dream of purity in a complex, toxic world.

Perhaps looking at #foodporn is a way to #eatclean? Indulging with eyes only, while the body remains a temple.

When people can choose between plenty and frugality the choice, whatever its motives, is a way of defining identity, declaring affinity, joining a community. In a world where so much overlaps and merges, extreme choices allure because they seem to offer a kind of distinction, which – especially online – means attention. Amidst all the virtual posting, sharing, liking, following, we tend to forget that something else is being eaten up – energy. The vast centres that house all our data consume colossal amounts of electricity. Soon they will be consuming a fifth of the earth's power, making them one of the biggest sources of pollution.

Whatever the preferred hashtag, all the imagery appears in some sort of online 'feed'. That word seems at once alien and apt in this context. These 'feeds', usually followed through a smartphone, are now part of the daily diet for many of us. Besides pictures of food, everything from news to art, sport to fashion, is being consumed, and more is then craved. Just how nourishing are these 'feeds'? Do they provide real sustenance or just empty calories? Perhaps it's not so much an issue of the content as of our inability to handle it. Studies abound of growing addiction to smartphones and its consequences, one of the most serious being the impact on relationships. We all know – or may be! – one of those who can't stop checking the mobile even when seated round the table for a meal with others. Doesn't matter who the host is then, because the ultimate host is the Internet hosting service keeping open the virtual doors to an endless supply of 'feeds', which all claim to be yours for 'free'. Be my guest, the Internet invites. It's hard to resist this generous host who offers so much, just for the price of all your web data. Yet, for being fed you become fodder.

I'M INTRIGUED BY ANOTHER carnal aspect of cuisine – the sense in which cooking can be a form of seduction. Variously coloured and shaped ingredients, different textures and spices combined to catch the eye, tease the nose, excite the palate, elicit sounds of pleasure. Food as an act of love that ends in consume-ation.

My greed, you see, extends to people as well. I always want to get that bit closer, have a little extra. I want to know more about those I find interesting or attractive, and sometimes even about those I dislike. I write partly to satisfy this hunger for others, for their most private thoughts and hidden selves. Writing allows you to press against an absolute stranger, to enter this person, to touch parts that even their closest intimates might not have reached. Sometimes the stranger dissolves and you see it is yourself you are holding, your own shadows being given substance, your own hidden longings coaxed into light.

Cooking also affords a measure of such remote yet close

contact. I used to note down in my diary what I cooked at every meal for guests, and I tried never to serve people the same thing twice. I no longer have the time or the same need to be so obsessive, but there's one friend for whom I always make something new. It's become the tradition of our eating together, the virgin dish. A never-ending 'first-time', a ritual of new sensations and their attendant reactions: laughter, delight, occasional ambivalence and, always, a special feeling as of a secret shared in public that nevertheless remains classified.

Food as flirting. Each course coyly flashing its parts, working its charms, caressing the tongue, titillating the taste buds. You eat, and all the while we talk about books, politics, back pain, holidays, everything. And only the odd sigh of pleasure reveals the other game that's simultaneously unfolding. Culinary coquetry. A little affair between your stomach and me.

One evening after a meal at our place my friend found her husband groaning in bed. 'What is it?' she asked.

'It's Priya!' He clutched his belly.

'You should have eaten less,' she said.

'How?' he huffed. 'It was too good!'

The frisson when I heard that story. Gratification all at once: instant, delayed, everlasting.

IN HER LECTURES ON Immanuel Kant's *Critique of Judgment*, Hannah Arendt too reflects, though rather differently to Brillat-Savarin, on taste and sense(s). Arendt explores Kant's thoughts on judgement, especially judgements of taste – in particular the ability to discern what is good or suitable.

The notion of the 'enlargement of the mind' is central to the *Critique of Judgment* (originally called *Critique of Taste*). Enlarged thought, according to Kant, is accomplished by 'comparing our judgment with the possible rather than the actual judgment of others, and by putting ourselves in the place of any other man'. For Kant, such judgements are based on a kind of *Sensus Communis*, which he prefers not to define merely as 'common sense', but rather as a *communal* sense.

Arendt elaborates on Kant's 'communal sense', describing it as an extra sense or mental capability that governs our understanding of community, emphasising Kant's view that a 'common understanding of men . . . is the very least to be expected from anyone claiming the name of man'.

Taste, Arendt finally construes, is a 'community sense' (*gemeinschaftlicher Sinn*) and she affirms Kant's assertion that 'sense' here means 'the effect of a reflection upon the mind'. Thought affects us as though it were a sensation.

'TASTE' IS ONE OF my favourite words. I love the sound, and the generous gamut it spans, from gustatory perception to judicious rumination. The expression 'acquired taste' has a particular charge for me. It refers to an appreciation for food or drink unlikely to be enjoyed by anyone who hasn't had much exposure to them, and which are rendered doubly strange by their strong smell, taste, or odd appearance. Dislike of things such as blue cheese, whisky, liquorice or durian is met by aficionados with a hint of condescension and a dash of pity. 'It's an acquired taste,' they will say, and some might add: 'The sign of a mature palate.' Reluctant to be excluded from supposedly wonderful, superior pleasures, or to remain immature, I've often wondered: how does one develop partiality for what is difficult or disliked?

Not easily, it seems. Changing preferences, whatever they might be, takes dedication and may even require pretence – doing something and telling yourself you like it until, perhaps, eventually you do.

ONE OF MY MOST prized possessions is a little bound volume of *Best Recipes* put together as a gift for me by my neighbours. All the seven families who live in our apartment block in Berlin did illustrated instructions on how to make their favourite dishes, many of which I have eaten at their homes with relish and tried, with varying degrees of success, to recreate in my own kitchen. The *Best Recipes* book is so precious because it reminds me of something I know but continually forget: a dish is not just the sum of its parts, it is its maker, its occasion, the company in which it is eaten. The food that's cooked for you is imbued with an ingredient no recipe can list, no culinary sleight of hand can substitute: hospitality. This is why, despite having learned how to make from scratch all the favourites amongst my mum's dishes, I still need the different batches of tarka from which to prepare versions at home. What you crave sometimes is not just a certain taste, but the presence – the touch – of a particular person or place.

THE ABILITY TO PUT oneself in the place of everyone else – the maxim of Kant's enlarged mentality – is also the foundation of hospitality, for it too usually extends from empathy. But hospitality can also be claimed, obliging us to be courteous, generous against our wishes.

In my extended Indian family, relatives – and everyone is somehow related, a cousin's cousin's cousin – always visited unannounced. If any of them disliked the practice, they never complained – at least not to each other's faces. It would have been shameful to show you were not in an ever-ready state of welcome. This was their community sense: deep but narrow. Possibly it enlarged now and then, I only know it shrank on the day of the UK's EU referendum, when many in my family voted for Brexit in the belief that it would stop more immigrants arriving in the country. Few imagined that halting this kind of movement, so deceptively simple, could stall so much else. Few envisaged that immigrants – unasked, unwanted – will always come, their arrival affirming a right to acknowledgement, their presence confirming a demand for decency, for humanity.

FOOD SUSTAINS US PHYSICALLY, yet to be fully nourished we must also be fed by ideas, feelings, experiences. Meeting over a meal perfectly combines these needs, nurturing on many levels, satisfying the mind as well as the soul and senses. Much as I adore a good dinner party, I also appreciate eating on my own while listening to a great podcast. Increasingly, I value occasions arranged purely to provide food for thought: readings, lectures, discussions, debates – situations that challenge convictions, that encourage courteous but rigorous verbal sparring.

I love the idea of the Ben Franklin Circles in the US. Named after Benjamin Franklin, one of America's founding fathers, these neighbourhood meet-ups are modelled on a weekly conversation club Franklin held with friends so they could discuss 'in the sincere spirit of inquiry after truth, without fondness for dispute, or desire of victory'. We urgently need more spaces where different kinds of people can meet face to face in such a spirit. In our age of widespread anonymity on internet platforms where exchanges can be so uncivil, the Ben Franklin Circles offer an alternative chat room in the belief that physically seeing and engaging with one another helps to foster deeper dialogue and a broader sense of community.

I long for such exchanges, request them, try to arrange them – and yet, even now, when a friend asks to bring someone I don't know to a dinner I've arranged my first reaction is: *Oh, no!* I resent the challenge to my plan for how things should be. Of course, in the end, I agree, and every single time it turns out perfectly fine. Once I said no, and the decision left a bad taste that still lingers: not only did the companion not come, neither did my friend.

Therein lies the conundrum of hospitality.

Without a guest, there is no host.

Without the host, no guest.

Only strangers.

I would like to thank:

Ulrike Ostermeyer, wonderful friend and editor, who planted the seeds for this book and made sure it found the right home.

Jonathan Landgrebe, who took a leap to publish an English book in German first.

Jamie Byng, who took on *Be My Guest* with the sort of passion and generosity a writer dreams of. Simon Thorogood, who edited with tremendous care and insight. Everyone at Canongate who got behind the book and did everything to help it on its way into the world. Sonny Mehta and Lexy Bloom, who received *Be My Guest* so enthusiastically at Knopf.

The Berlin Senate Department for Culture and Europe, who gave me freedom in the form of a stipendium.

Susanne Fladt-Bruno, who helped me feel more at home in the German language.

The women at WIR MACHEN DAS with whom I have worked, above all, Annika Reich – exemplary friend and host.

Bernhard Robben, Rima Chammaa, Adania Shibli, Pepe Egger, Patricia Breves, Rafael Cardoso, Emma Tingey,

Martin Crook, Gabrielle von Arnim and Doris D'Cruz-Grote – for delicious meals and the enduring nourishment of friendship.

Madeleine Thien, Rawi Hage, Philipp Ostrowicz, Amanda Michalopoulou and Gail Jones – whose regular returns to Berlin make it bigger and brighter for me.

Ulrich Schreiber, who welcomes ideas and initiatives like no one else I know: working with him has opened up many worlds.

Frank Berberich, who gave me space to stretch myself in *Lettre International*: those essays were the path to this book.

My house-family – the neighbours whose generosity itself is home.

My Lübeck-family – Edda and Jana, Hans and Barbara, who always insist on inviting me.

My family – Pa, Agam, Nef, Mumji and especially my mum Gudy, my sister Seema and my niece Lara – their love sustains me across the starvation of distance.

Eve Lucas and Lina Meruane – cherished friends and first readers. This book is the better for their insight.

Beatrice Faßbender – peerless friend and translator – for reading with forensic eyes and deep feeling.

Matti – for all the give and take, every day and beyond.

Bibliography

The Human Condition, by Hannah Arendt – The University of
Chicago Press, Chicago, 1998

The Life of the Mind, by Hannah Arendt (Excerpts from
Lectures on Kant's Political Philosophy) – Harcourt,
San Diego, 1978

Agriculture: A Very Short Introduction, by Paul Brassley and Richard
Soffe – Oxford University Press, Oxford, 2016

The Physiology of Taste, by Jean Anthelme Brillat-Savarin –
translated from the last Paris edition by Fayette Robinson,
eBooks@Adelaide The University of Adelaide Library,
Adelaide, 2014

Stigmata, by Hélène Cixous – Routledge, Oxon, 1998

*The Hungry Empire, How Britain's Quest for Food Shaped the Modern
World*, by Lizzie Collingham – The Bodley Head, Vintage
Publishing, London, 2017

*Late Victorian Holocausts, El Niño Famines and the Making of the Third
World*, by Mike Davis – Verso, London and New York,
2001

'From the Word to Life: A Dialogue between Jacques Derrida and Hélène Cixous' by Jacques Derrida, Hélène Cixous, Aliette Armel and Ashley Thompson. *New Literary History* 37, no. 1 — John Hopkins University Press, Baltimore, 2006

Cultural Memory in the Present: Of Hospitality, Anne Dufourmantelle Invites Jacques Derrida to Respond — Stanford University Press, Stanford, 2000

The Critique of Judgment, by Immanuel Kant — translated with introduction and notes by J.H. Bernard (2nd ed. revised), Macmillan, London, 1914

A Moveable Feast, Ten Millennia of Food Globalization, by Kenneth F. Kiple — Cambridge University Press, Cambridge, 2007

Food: A Very Short Introduction, by John Krebs — Oxford University Press, Oxford, 2013

Leere Töpfe, volle Töpfe — Die Kulturgeschichte des Essens und Trinkens Gert V. Paczensky, Anna Duennebier — Albrecht Knaus Verlag, Munich, 1994

Globalization: A Very Short Introduction, by Manfred B. Stegner — Oxford University Press, Oxford, 2017